# holiday touches
## for the
# country
# home

*A few well-chosen decorations always help to set the mood for our special celebrations. With appealing accessories, each event becomes an opportunity to express our feelings about the day or those it honors. Perhaps it's the fun that such decorating brings to our lives that inspires us to dress up our homes, not just for Christmas but all through the year.*

*Filled with reminders of our rich American heritage, the country home is the perfect setting for observing our time-honored holiday traditions. To help you enjoy these days to the fullest, we've created this book of simple keepsakes, gifts, and decorations to blend with your country furnishings and collectibles. These delightful touches — many of which can be left out all year — will fill your home with warmth and help you create wonderful memories for family and friends!*

*Anne Young*

**LEISURE ARTS**
Little Rock, Arkansas

# holiday touches
## for the
# country home

MEMORIES IN THE MAKING SERIES

Printed in the United States of America. First Printing. International Standard Book Number 0-942237-06-4

## EDITORIAL STAFF

**Editor-in-Chief:** Anne Van Wagner Young
**Managing Editor:** Sandra Graham Case
**Creative Art Director:** Gloria Hodgson
**Assistant Editor:** Susan Frantz Wiles

**PRODUCTION**
**Production Director:** Jane Kenner Prather
**Production Assistants:** Sherry Taylor O'Connor, Kathy Rose Bradley, Micah Land, and Diana Heien Suttle

**EDITORIAL**
**Editorial Director:** Dorothy Latimer Johnson
**Editorial Assistants:** Linda L. Trimble, Marjorie Lacy Bishop, Tammi Foress Williamson, Tena Kelley Vaughn, and Darla Burdette Kelsay

**ART**
**Production Art Director:** Melinda Stout
**Production Artist:** Linda Lovette
**Art Production Assistants:** Diane M. Hugo, Leslie Loring Krebs, Kathleen Murphy, Cindy Nassab, and Mike States
**Photo Stylist:** Karen Smart Hall
**Typesetters:** Laura Glover Burris and Vicky Fielder Evans

## BUSINESS STAFF

**Publisher:** Steve Patterson
**Controller:** Tom Siebenmorgen
**Retail Sales Director:** Richard Tignor
**Retail Marketing Director:** Pam Stebbins
**Retail Customer Services Director:** Margaret Sweetin
**Marketing Manager:** Russ Barnett
**Circulation Manager:** Guy A. Crossley
**Print Production Manager:** Chris Schaefer

# TABLE OF CONTENTS

# TABLE OF CONTENTS
(Continued)

# Thanksgiving . . . . . . . . . . . . . . 86

# Christmas . . . . . . . . . . . . . . . . 96

# General Instructions . . . . . . . . . . . . . . . 124

# Credits . . . . . . . . . . . . . . . . . . . 127

# Valentine's Day

On this day of romance,
fragrant roses and thoughtful
remembrances touch the sentimental
chords in our hearts. We treasure
the timeless charm of Valentine's Day,
savoring the warmth and beauty it
brings to our lives. Cherished
memories and mementos
are tenderly recalled and unwrapped
during this special time, and
we set our hands to crafting new
valentine keepsakes as well.
By decorating our homes
with symbols of love,
we share this wonderful experience
with family and friends.

Instructions for this collection begin on page 14.

$\mathcal{R}$oses turn our thoughts to romance, whether they're lovingly gathered and preserved with time or captured with needle and thread. Delicate buds from a special bouquet transform a tiny wreath into a treasured remembrance. A soft, embroidered afghan and pillow invite sweet daydreams. And an elegantly penned scripture expresses the everlasting qualities of true love.

*elieving that anything useful should also be beautiful, the Victorians embellished everything, especially such personal items as letter boxes. Sure to be among the cherished correspondence kept inside were handmade valentines — then, as now, a very special way to say "I love you."*

A graceful crescent adorned with roses adds romance to a bedroom, transforming it into a lovely boudoir. Here, matters of the heart become the fabric of dreams.

*ittle touches of romance tucked in unexpected places bring beauty to our homes — sweet-smelling roses on a wreath or in a basket, linens adorned with elegant monograms, a shelf edged with lacy paper hearts. In a color-washed paper mobile, we see the revival of a lovely Victorian art form.*

# OLD-FASHIONED DOLL (Shown on page 7)

*For doll,* you will need two 6" x 9" pieces of white poplin fabric; tracing paper; polyester fiberfill; thread to match fabric; instant coffee; Folk Art® acrylic paint (see Step 6 for colors); a soft cloth; fabric marking pencil; small, flat paintbrush; foam brush; black, red, and brown permanent felt-tip pens with fine points; pink, red, and brown colored pencils; 6" of 1⁄16"w satin ribbon; and craft glue.

1. Dissolve 1 tablespoon instant coffee in 1 cup hot water. Soak fabric pieces in coffee several minutes. Remove from coffee and allow to dry; press.
2. Trace doll pattern, page 15, onto tracing paper and cut out.
3. Place fabric pieces right sides together. Center pattern on top of pieces and use fabric marking pencil to draw around pattern. DO NOT CUT OUT SHAPE. Carefully sew pieces together directly on pencil line. Leaving a 1⁄4" seam allowance, cut out doll; clip curves.
4. Cut a 2" long slit through center back of doll; turn right side out. Lightly stuff arms and legs with fiberfill. Machine sew along tops of arms and legs where indicated by dashed lines on pattern. Firmly stuff body; sew final closure by hand.
5. (Note: Refer to photo for Steps 5 - 10.) Referring to pattern, use a lead pencil to lightly mark placement of hair, clothing, shoes, and facial features.
6. (Note: Paint back of doll to correspond with front of doll.) To paint doll, dilute Almond Parfait paint with water to produce a thin wash resembling watercolor; use flat paintbrush and paint face, arms, and legs. Allow to dry. Use the following colors to paint doll:
   Vanilla Cream - clothing
   Buttercrunch - hair
   Butter Pecan - shoes

Allow to dry.

7. Referring to pattern, use brown pen to draw lace on clothing, details on shoes, and lines for hair. Use black pen and a light dotting motion to draw eyes and nose; use red pen and repeat for mouth.
8. Use pink pencil to blush cheeks, brown pencil to color eyes, and red pencil to color mouth.
9. To antique doll, dilute Butter Pecan with water to produce a thin wash resembling watercolor. Use foam brush to paint entire doll; remove excess with soft cloth. Allow to dry.
10. Tie ribbon in a bow; trim ends. Glue bow to hair.

*For dress,* you will need one 16" square of unbleached cotton muslin, 5" of 1⁄2"w lace trim, instant coffee, thread to match fabric, two 1⁄8" snaps, 13 1⁄2" of 1"w lace trim, and 15" of 1⁄16"w ribbon.

1. Dissolve 1 tablespoon instant coffee in 1 cup hot water. Soak muslin in coffee several minutes. Remove from coffee and allow to dry; press.
2. From muslin, cut one 7 1⁄2" x 11" piece for front and two 3 1⁄2" x 11" pieces for back.
3. Beginning 1⁄4" from one short edge of front piece (top), machine baste six straight lines 1⁄4" apart (Fig. 1); repeat for back pieces.

Fig. 1

4. Pull basting threads to gather front piece to 3" wide; knot threads. Repeat to gather each back piece to 1 1⁄2" wide; knot threads.
5. Matching right sides and long edges, place one back piece on front piece. Beginning below gathered area and using a 1⁄4" seam allowance, sew pieces together. Press seam open and at the same time press edges of gathered areas 1⁄4" to wrong side. Repeat to attach remaining back piece.
6. For armholes, refer to dashed lines in Fig. 2 and stitch edges in place. Refer to dotted lines in Fig. 2 and baste top edges of armholes together.

Fig. 2

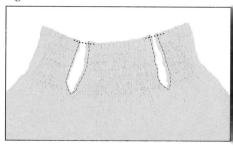

7. Fold remaining long edge of each back piece 1⁄4" to wrong side; press. Stitch in place.
8. Fold short edges of 1⁄2" wide lace trim 1⁄4" to wrong side. With wrong sides together, fold lace in half lengthwise; press. Insert top edge of dress between folded edges of lace; hand sew lace in place.
9. For tucks, fold bottom edge of dress 1 3⁄8" to wrong side; press. Stitch 1⁄8" from folded edge. Press seam open. Repeat two times, folding bottom edge 1 3⁄4" and then 2 1⁄8" to wrong side. Press tucks toward bottom of dress.
10. Fold short edges of 1" wide lace trim 1⁄4" to wrong side; press. Matching right sides and long edges, use a 1⁄4" seam allowance and sew lace to bottom of dress; press.
11. Sew snaps to back of dress at neck and waist.
12. Tie ribbon in a bow. Referring to photo, tack bow to dress.

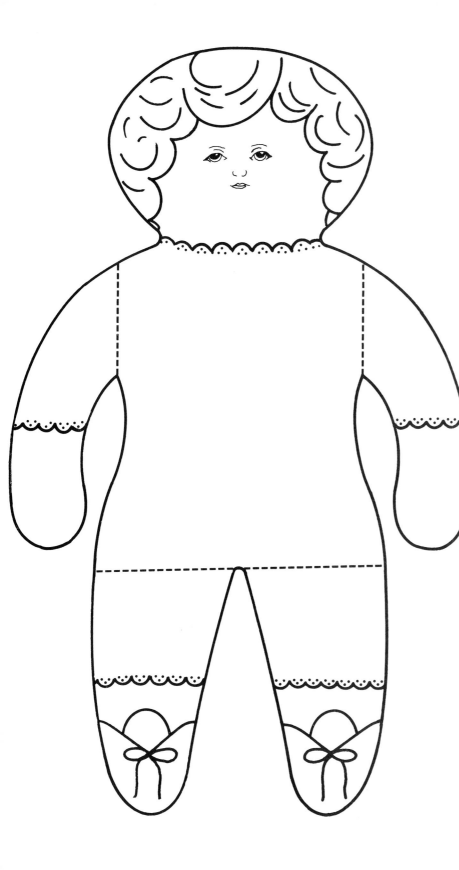

## KEEPSAKE ROSE WREATH
(Shown on page 12)

*You will need* dried long-stemmed roses (see Note below), dried natural baby's breath, dried plumosa fern, grapevine wreath, grosgrain ribbon, florist wire, wire cutters, hot glue gun, and glue sticks.

Note: We used purchased dried roses, but you may dry your own. Tie fresh roses together in a bundle and hang upside down in a dark, dry place for several weeks until dry. Or dry the roses in silica gel following manufacturer's instructions.

1. (Note: Refer to photo to assemble wreath.) Wire rose stems together. Wire roses to wreath.
2. Glue baby's breath and fern among roses.
3. Use ribbon to make a multi-loop bow. Wire bow to rose stems.

## ROSE CRESCENT
(Shown on page 11)

*You will need* one 14" dia. plastic foam wreath base, Spanish moss, dried long-stemmed roses (see Note in Keepsake Rose Wreath instructions on this page), dried natural baby's breath, approx. 9" long twigs cut from a twig wreath, utility knife, wire cutters, florist wire, hot glue gun, and glue sticks.

1. To form crescent, use utility knife to cut away approximately one-quarter of wreath base. Glue Spanish moss over entire base.
2. (Note: Refer to photo to assemble crescent.) Insert twigs into base; glue to secure.
3. Remove leaves from rose stems and set aside. Trim stems approximately 4" long. Glue roses and baby's breath to wreath. Glue leaves to wreath.
4. Use wire to form a hanger on back of wreath.

15

# CHERUB MOBILE (Shown on page 12)

*You will need* medium weight ivory paper (cover stock); acrylic paint (refer to photo for colors); small paintbrushes; heavy thread (buttonhole twist); large, sharp needle; tracing paper; craft glue; brown colored pencil; and graphite transfer paper.

1. Trace patterns onto tracing paper. Use transfer paper to transfer patterns onto ivory paper; cut out.
2. (Note: Refer to photo for Steps 2 - 8.) Dilute paint with water to produce a thin wash resembling watercolor. Paint front of each cherub. Paint hair on back of each cherub. Paint remaining area of each cherub same color as wings; allow to dry.
3. Paint both sides of dove and small and medium hearts. Paint both sides of hearts on hands. Paint hearts on envelope (see Fig. 1 for back).

Fig. 1

4. Use colored pencil to write "Be Mine" on each cherub heart, to print address on envelope, and to draw flap on back of envelope.
5. Use needle to pierce holes where indicated by dots on wings.
6. Matching front of wings, fold each cherub in half. Glue cherubs together along folds.
7. (Note: Use needle and thread to assemble mobile. Knot ends of thread to secure.) Hang small heart 1½" below medium heart. Hang medium heart 3½" below heart on cherub. Hang remaining shapes 3½" below wings.
8. For hanger, thread 8" of thread through top of mobile and knot ends of thread together.

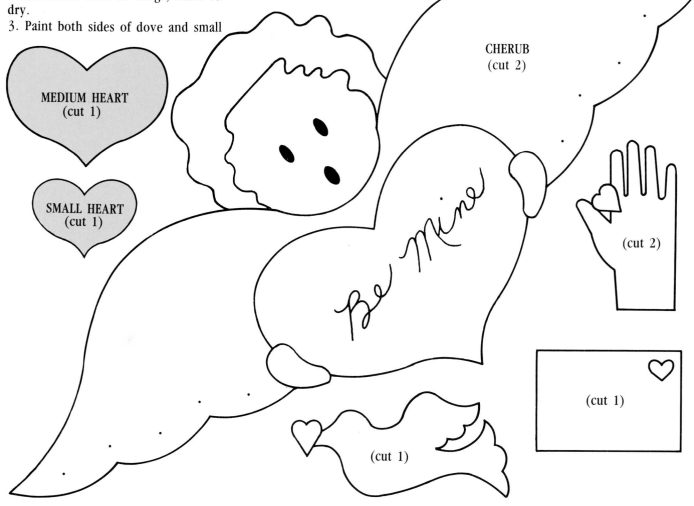

## LOVE VERSE
(Shown on page 9)

*You will need* one 8″ x 10″ piece of natural parchment paper; dried natural baby's breath; 24″ of $\frac{1}{16}$″w ribbon; purchased small, dried roses; black felt-tip calligraphy pen with fine point; 8″ x 10″ frame (we used a custom frame); hot glue gun; and glue sticks.

1. Center paper over pattern and use a pencil to lightly trace outline of heart. Use pen to trace verse onto paper.
2. Glue small pieces of baby's breath along pencil line. Use ribbon to make a 2½″ wide multi-loop bow with approximately 8″ long streamers. Knot ends of streamers. Referring to photo, glue roses and bow to baby's breath.
3. Insert in frame.

## VICTORIAN LETTER BOX  (Shown on page 10)

*You will need* one wooden box, acrylic paint, motifs cut from gift wrap, one verse cut from a greeting card, matte Mod Podge™ sealer, fruitwood water-based stain, #400 wet/dry sandpaper, paintbrushes, and a soft cloth.

1. Paint box; allow to dry. Arrange verse and motifs on box lid as desired. Use sealer to glue verse and motifs to box lid; allow to dry.
2. Apply stain to entire project and remove excess with soft cloth; allow to dry.
3. Apply five coats of sealer to box, allowing to dry between coats.
4. Use sandpaper to wet-sand box, smoothing any ridges or bubbles.

Love beareth all things, believeth all things, hopeth all things, endureth all things. Love never ends...

I Corinthians 13:7-8

## ROMANTIC PAPER EDGING
(Shown on page 13)

*You will need* natural parchment paper; small, sharp scissors; craft knife; large, sharp needle; tracing paper; graphite transfer paper; removable tape; transparent tape; cutting mat or thick layer of newspapers; and a small terry towel.

1. Trace paper edging pattern onto tracing paper.
2. Cut one 8½″ x 9″ length of parchment paper. Fold one short edge 2¼″ to one side. Using fold as a guide, fanfold remaining length of paper. Use removable tape to hold edges of paper together.
3. With bottom of pattern ½″ from one short edge of folded paper, use transfer paper to transfer pattern to folded paper.
4. Use craft knife to cut out paper along grey lines. Use scissors to cut out paper along solid black lines. Unfold paper and press with a warm, dry iron.
5. For pierced areas, place edging on folded towel and use needle to pierce holes where indicated by dots.
6. Repeat Steps 2 - 5 for desired number of lengths. Use transparent tape to tape lengths of edging together. Fold edging where indicated by dashed line at top of pattern.

## PIERCED PAPER HEARTS   (Shown on page 7)

*You will need* medium weight ivory paper (cover stock); tracing paper; graphite transfer paper; large, sharp needle; craft knife; small, sharp scissors; small terry towel; rubber cutting mat or thick layer of newspapers; and craft glue and nylon line (for hangers).

1. Trace desired heart patterns onto tracing paper. Use transfer paper to transfer patterns onto ivory paper; cut out.
2. For pierced areas, place each heart on folded towel and use needle to pierce holes where indicated by dots.
3. For cutouts or lines on heart 2, 3, or 4, place each heart on cutting mat and use craft knife to cut details.
4. For each hanger, cut one 2″ length of nylon line; glue ends to top center of heart on wrong side (smooth side).

1.

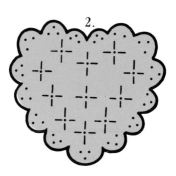

2.

# VALENTINES

(Shown on page 10)

*You will need* medium weight ivory paper (cover stock); tracing paper; graphite transfer paper; large, sharp needle; small, sharp scissors; small terry towel; pen with brown ink; and envelopes to fit valentines.

1. Use valentine patterns and follow Steps 1 and 2 of Pierced Paper Hearts instructions, page 18, to make valentines.
2. Referring to photo, use pen to write desired messages on valentines.

# HEARTFELT WREATH

(Shown on page 9)

*You will need* dried roses (see Note in Keepsake Rose Wreath instructions, page 15), dried natural baby's breath, dried plumosa fern, heart-shaped grapevine wreath, satin ribbon, hot glue gun, and glue sticks.

1. Referring to photo, glue roses, baby's breath, and fern to wreath.
2. Use ribbon to make a multi-loop bow. Glue bow to wreath.

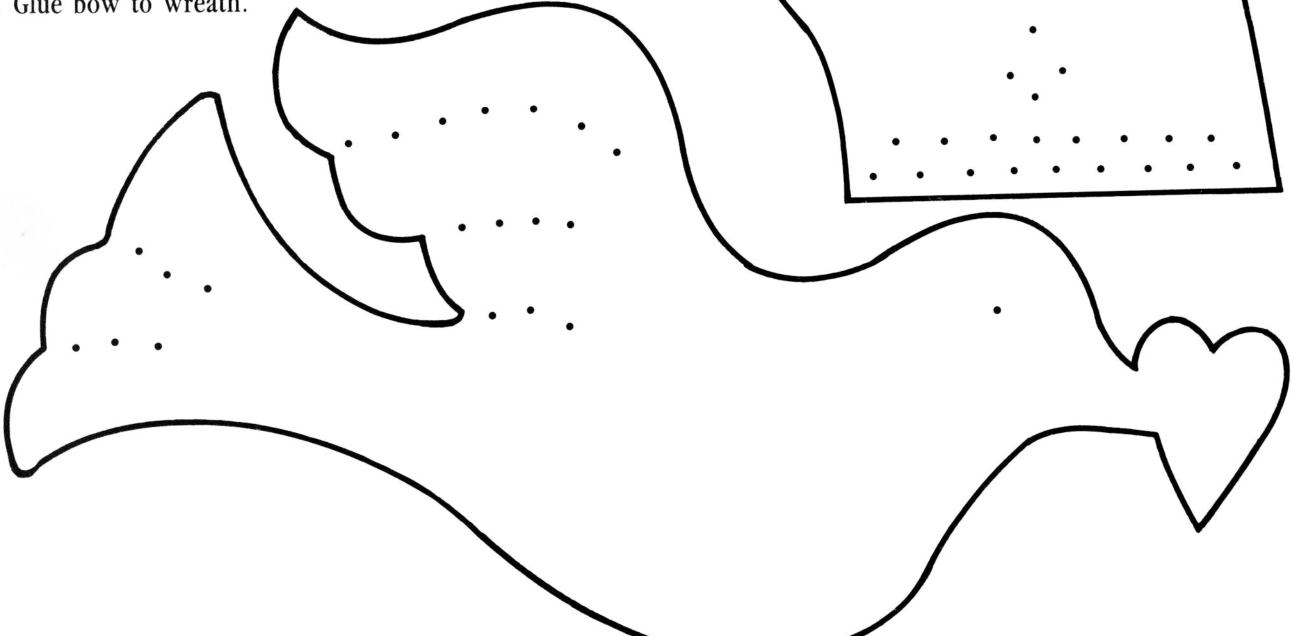

## POTPOURRI OF ROSES
(Shown on page 13)

*You will need* fresh rose blossoms and leaves, silica gel, rose essential oil, Spanish moss, and desired container to hold potpourri.

1. Following manufacturer's instructions, dry roses and leaves in silica gel.
2. Line container with Spanish moss. Arrange dried roses and leaves on top of Spanish moss.
3. Sprinkle potpourri with several drops of essential oil. Additional oil may be added as needed.

## MONOGRAMMED TOWEL
(Shown on page 13)

*You will need* one 13″ x 19½″ piece of Cream Belfast Linen (32 ct), sewing thread to match linen, embroidery floss (see color key, page 21), 13″ of 1¾″w lace trim, embroidery hoop (optional), and grid paper and removable tape for charting initials (optional).

Note: Since different combinations of letters require different spacing, you may want to chart and space your initials first on grid paper before beginning to stitch. Chart each letter on grid paper; cut letters apart. Place letters on grid paper and adjust spacing; tape in place.

1. With bottoms of initials 2″ from one short edge of fabric, follow Working On Linen, page 125, to work initials, page 21, over two fabric threads. Use 2 strands of floss for Cross Stitch.
2. Fold long edges of fabric under ¼″ and press; fold under ¼″ again and hem. Fold short edges under ¼″ and press; fold under ½″ again and hem.
3. Fold short edges of trim under ½″. Sew trim to bottom edge of towel.

## WREATH OF ROSES AFGHAN
(Shown on page 8)

*You will need* 1¼ yds of Ivory Anne Cloth (18 ct), embroidery floss (see color key, page 21), embroidery hoop (optional), and grid paper and removable tape for charting initials (optional).

1. To fringe afghan, cut off selvages; fabric should measure 45″ x 58″. Measure 5½″ from one raw edge of fabric and pull out one fabric thread. Pull out threads up to missing fabric thread. Repeat for each edge.
2. Using overhand knots, begin by tying a knot at each corner with four hortizontal and four vertical threads (Fig. 1). Then working from corners, use eight fabric threads for each knot until all threads are knotted.

Fig. 1

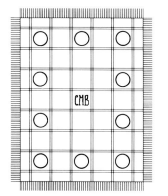

3. Refer to Diagram for placement of wreaths and initials. For initials, refer to Note in Monogrammed Towel instructions on this page. Work each design over two fabric threads, using 6 strands of floss for Cross Stitch.

DIAGRAM

## WREATH OF ROSES PILLOW
(Shown on page 8)

*You will need* two 9″ squares of Cream Belfast Linen (32 ct), sewing thread to match linen, 1⅔ yds of $\frac{1}{16}$″w ribbon and embroidery floss to match, embroidery floss (see color key, page 21), embroidery hoop (optional), and polyester fiberfill.

1. On one fabric piece, follow Working On Linen, page 125, to work wreath, page 21, over two fabric threads. Use 2 strands of floss for Cross Stitch.
2. For ribbon trim, refer to photo and begin 16″ from one end of ribbon; pin ribbon 2″ from design. Use 1 strand of floss to Cross Stitch over ribbon (Fig. 1). Remove pins.

Fig. 1

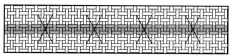

3. For pillow, place fabric pieces right sides together. Leaving an opening for turning, sew ½″ from all edges. Trim seam allowance to ¼″ and cut corners diagonally. Turn right side out; press. Leaving an opening for stuffing across from existing opening, use zipper foot and machine stitch close to outer edge of ribbon (Fig. 2). Stuff center area only with fiberfill. Machine stitch inner opening closed.

Fig. 2

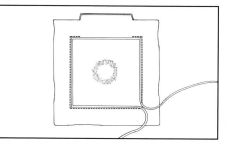

4. Sew final closure by hand.
5. Tie ribbon in a bow; trim ends even.

WREATH (33w x 33h)
ALPHABET

| X | DMC | ANC. | COLOR |
|---|------|------|-------|
| ▲ | 501 | 0878 | dk green |
| ☉ | 502 | 0876 | green |
| ◇ | 524 | 0875 | lt green |
| ✳ | 610 | 0889 | brown |
| ⊙ | 760 | 09 | rose |
| – | 761 | 08 | lt rose |
| ✶ | 816 | 044 | vy dk rose |
| ✕ | 3328 | 011 | dk rose |

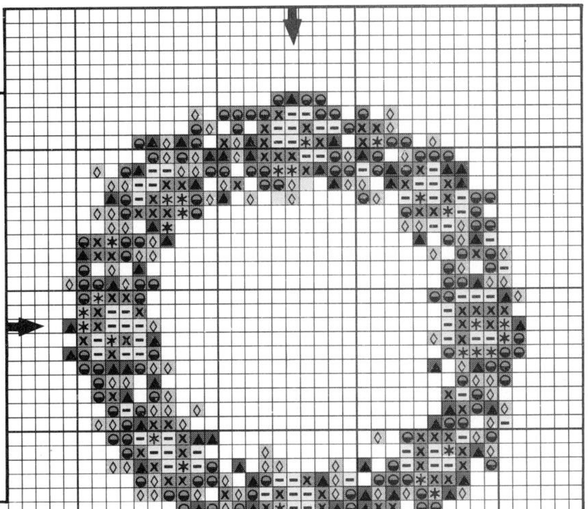

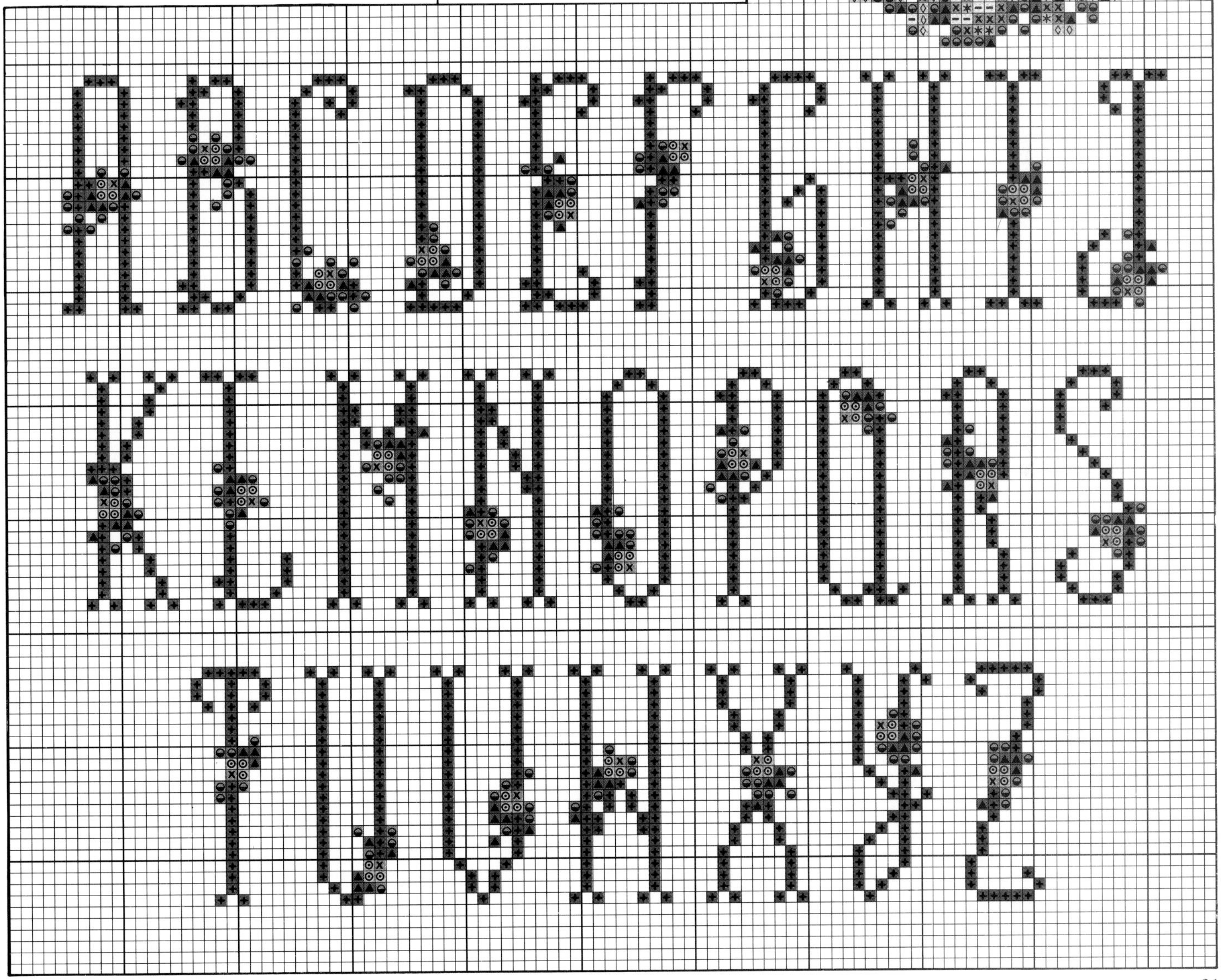

21

# St. Patrick's Day

*There's something captivating about the rich folklore of Ireland, where the miraculous deeds of saints are recorded alongside the mischievous pranks of leprechauns and fairies — and the pot of gold at the rainbow's end is always just beyond the next hill. On St. Patrick's Day, we all become a little bit Irish as we revel in the customs of these fun-loving people. The hope of good fortune and friendship, often expressed in Irish blessings, is at the heart of this happy celebration.*

Instructions for this collection begin on page 25.

*T*he gentle beauty of
this little Irish Chain
quilt evokes images of
Ireland's soft mists
and rolling green hills.
A quilted cable pattern
makes a pretty border,
and traditional
shamrock shapes
enhance the Irish
mood.

## SHAMROCK SWEATSHIRT   (Shown on this page)

*You will need* one white sweatshirt, green and black fabric paint, one 6″ x 3½″ x 1″ cellulose sponge, cardboard to fit snugly inside body of sweatshirt, round paintbrush, tracing paper, foam brush, and a pressing cloth.

1. Wash and dry sweatshirt. Place cardboard inside sweatshirt.
2. Trace leaf and stem patterns onto tracing paper and cut out. Use patterns and cut one leaf and one stem from sponge.
3. Dampen sponge pieces and squeeze out excess water.
4. (Note: Practice stamping technique on paper before stamping sweatshirt.)

Reapplying paint after each stamp, use foam brush to apply an even coat of green paint to sponge pieces. For each shamrock, refer to photo and stamp three leaves and one stem on sweatshirt. Repeat to stamp desired number of shamrocks; allow to dry.
5. (Note: Practice slinging technique before applying paint to sweatshirt. Protect surfaces and clothing from paint.) Load paintbrush with black paint. Using a sharp, slinging motion, sling paint onto sweatshirt. Repeat as desired. Allow to dry.
6. Heat set design by using pressing cloth and a hot, dry iron.

*The "wearin' o' the green" is a fun way to display Irish pride.*

## IRISH CHAIN WALL HANGING
(Shown on page 24)

*You will need* ½ yd of green 44″w cotton fabric, 1⅛ yds of white 44″w cotton fabric, 1⅛ yds of 44″w cotton fabric for backing and hanging sleeve, ¾ yd of 44″w cotton fabric for bias binding, one 36″ x 45″ piece of low-loft polyester bonded batting, white thread, tracing paper, dressmaker's carbon, quilting needle, white quilting thread, quilting hoop, and one 28½″ length of ½″ dia. wooden dowel.

Note: For each sewing step, pin fabric pieces right sides together, matching raw edges; use a ¼″ seam allowance throughout.

1. Wash, dry, and press all fabrics. Trim selvages from fabrics.
2. For panel A, cut two 2″ x 25″ pieces from green fabric and one 5″ x 25″ piece from white fabric. Matching long edges, sew pieces together, alternating green and white fabrics. Press seam allowances toward green fabric.
3. For panel B, cut one 8″ x 31″ piece from white fabric.
4. Cutting across the width of each panel, cut twelve 2″ wide strips from panel A and six 5″ wide strips from panel B.
5. For one Block #1, refer to Fig. 1, page 26, and sew two strips from panel A and one strip from panel B together. Press seam allowances away from center of block. Repeat to make a total of six blocks.

Continued on page 26

Fig. 1

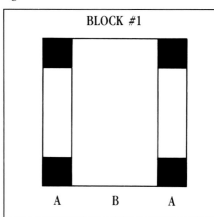

BLOCK #1

A     B     A

6. Cut five 2″ x 44″ pieces each from white and green fabrics. For panel C, sew three white pieces and two green pieces together, alternating white and green pieces. For panel D, sew three green pieces and two white pieces together, alternating green and white pieces. Press seam allowances toward green fabric.

7. Cutting across the width of each panel, cut eighteen 2″ wide strips from panel C and twelve 2″ wide strips from panel D.

8. For one Block #2, refer to Fig. 2 and sew three strips from panel C and two strips from panel D together. Press seam allowances in one direction. Repeat to make a total of six blocks.

Fig. 2

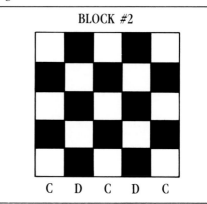

BLOCK #2

C   D   C   D   C

9. (Note: Refer to Diagram for Steps 9 - 13.) To assemble quilt top,

sew blocks into four rows; press seam allowances in one direction. Sew rows together; press seam allowances in one direction.

10. For borders, cut four 3½″ squares from green fabric. From white fabric, cut two fabric strips 3½″ wide and the length of the quilt top and two strips 3½″ wide and the width of the quilt top.

11. For side borders, sew one of the longer white strips to each long edge of the quilt top. Press seam allowances toward borders.

12. For top border, sew one green square to each short edge of one of the remaining white strips. For bottom border, repeat with remaining pieces. Press seam allowances toward green fabric. Sew borders to top and bottom edges of quilt top. Press seam allowances toward borders.

13. Trace shamrock quilting pattern onto tracing paper. Use dressmaker's carbon to transfer shamrock pattern onto center of each Block #1; transfer one leaf of shamrock pattern onto each corner block of border for heart. Trace cable quilting pattern onto tracing paper, repeating pattern to fit on white fabric of borders. Transfer cable pattern onto borders.

14. Cut backing fabric and batting 1½″ larger on all sides than quilt top. Place batting on wrong side of backing. Center quilt top, right side up, on batting. Smoothing any wrinkles in the quilt top, pin all layers together. Baste layers together from corner to corner and from side to side; remove pins.

15. Insert basted layers in hoop, pulling materials taut. Begin quilting in the center, then work clockwise toward the edges of the quilt. Use quilting thread and Quilting Stitch, page 126, to quilt shamrocks, hearts, and cables; quilt ''in the ditch'' (close to seamlines) around each block and along diagonal lines at center of chain

(indicated by dashed lines on Diagram).

16. Trim batting and backing even with quilt top. Remove basting threads and markings.

17. For hanging sleeve, cut a piece of fabric 6″ wide and 1″ shorter than the width of the quilt. Fold short edges ¼″ to wrong side and press; fold ¼″ to wrong side again and machine stitch close to folded edges. Matching wrong sides and raw edges, fold fabric in half lengthwise and press. Matching raw edges of sleeve with raw edges at top of quilt, center sleeve on backing fabric; use a ¼″ seam allowance and baste sleeve to top of quilt. Whipstitch fold of sleeve to backing.

18. (Note: When applying binding to edges of quilt, treat hanging sleeve as part of backing, enclosing all raw edges in binding.) For binding, cut one 1½″ x 140″ bias strip from binding fabric (piece as necessary). Follow Applying Binding, page 126, to finish edges of quilt. Insert dowel into hanging sleeve.

DIAGRAM

# AN IRISH BLESSING (Shown on page 23)

*You will need* one 12″ square of Cream Lugana (25 ct), embroidery floss (see color key), embroidery hoop (optional), and desired frame (we used a custom frame).

1. Work design over two fabric threads, using 3 strands of floss for Cross Stitch, 1 for Backstitch, and 1 for French Knots.
2. Frame as desired.

| AN IRISH BLESSING | (90w x 75h) |
|---|---|
| Aida 11 | 8¼″ x 6⅞″ |
| Aida 14 | 6½″ x 5⅜″ |
| Aida 18 | 5″ x 4¼″ |
| Hardanger 22 | 4⅛″ x 3½″ |

## AN IRISH BLESSING (90w x 75h)

| X | DMC | ¼X | B'ST | ANC. | COLOR | X | DMC | ¼X | B'ST | ANC. | COLOR | X | DMC | ¼X | B'ST | ANC. | COLOR |
|---|---|---|---|---|---|---|---|---|---|---|---|---|---|---|---|---|---|
|  | blanc |  |  | 02 | white | + | 927 |  |  | 0848 | lt grey | x | 988 |  |  | 0257 | lt green |
| O | 744 |  |  | 0293 | yellow | S | 986 |  |  | 0245 | dk green | ◇ | 989 |  |  | 0268 | vy lt green |
|  | 895 |  |  | 0246 | vy dk green | ▲ | 987 |  |  | 0258 | green | • | 895 |  |  |  | vy dk green French Knot |

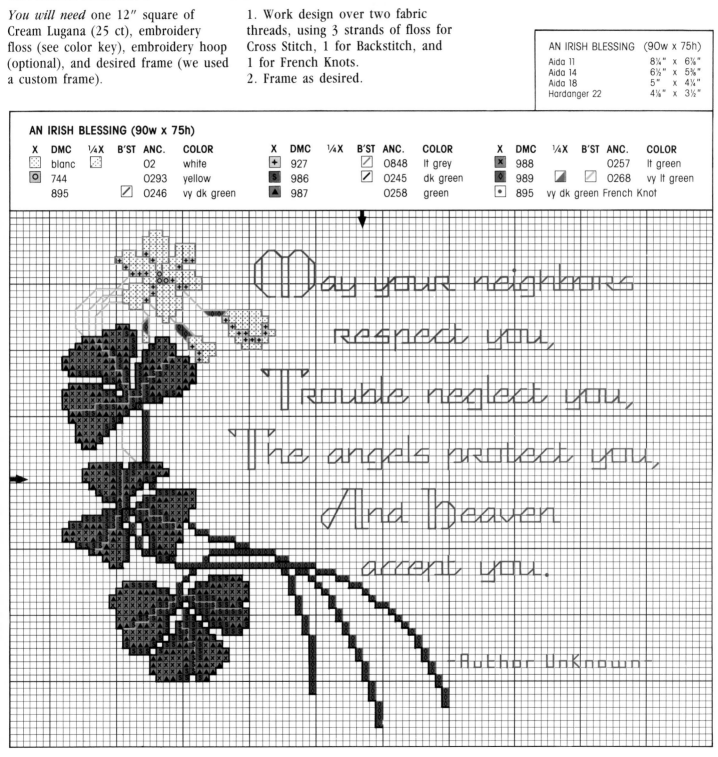

May your neighbors respect you, Trouble neglect you, The angels protect you, And heaven accept you.

-Author UnKnown-

# EASTER

Amid the miracle of the earth's spring renewal, Easter brings a celebration of new life. The retelling of the Resurrection story strengthens our hope and faith, and we draw our families close to share the joy in our hearts. As we delight the children with colored eggs and tales of the Easter bunny, we experience a gladness unlike that found at any other time of year.

Instructions for this collection begin on page 38.

E aster arrives just as the earth comes alive with spring flowers and baby animals. As Bibles are opened to the Easter story, where the Cross is a central element, the precious gift of life takes on special significance.

*C*hocolate bunnies have delighted generations of children at Eastertime. Now by using replicas of antique chocolate molds, we can craft paper bunnies to link us to those Easter celebrations gone by.

*Viewed as symbols of life, eggs have been traditional springtime gifts since ancient times. The legend that the eggs are brought by the Easter bunny began several centuries ago in Germany. According to folklore, a mother hid some colored eggs in a nest of straw as an Easter surprise for her children. Just as the youngsters found the nest, they spied a large rabbit hopping away and quickly concluded that the rabbit must have delivered the beautiful eggs. This year, wouldn't it be fun to thank this generous rabbit by leaving his favorite treat (carrots!) on the porch or on a peg by the door!*

# ANTIQUED EGG
(Shown on page 37)

*You will need* one 9″ long plastic egg with flat base and clear, removable top; ivory acrylic paint; desired color Paper Capers™ twisted paper; dried flowers and greenery; hot glue gun; glue sticks; newspaper; craft glue; gesso; foam brushes; medium sandpaper; a soft cloth; and fruitwood water-based stain.

1. Tear newspaper into approximately ¾″ x 3″ strips.
2. In a medium bowl, mix 2 parts craft glue and 1 part water. Dip strips in glue and pull between two fingers to remove excess glue. Wrap strips around egg, smoothing wrinkles with fingers. Overlapping strips, continue wrapping until egg is covered; allow to dry.
3. Apply two coats of gesso to egg, allowing to dry between coats.
4. Lightly sand egg to smooth surface. Remove sanding dust with a damp cloth.
5. Paint egg; allow to dry.
6. Apply stain to egg and remove excess with soft cloth; allow to dry.
7. (Note: Refer to photo to decorate egg. Use hot glue in Steps 7 and 8.) For bow, cut three 1″ x 15″ pieces and one 1″ x 2½″ piece from untwisted paper. Overlapping short edges ¼″, form each 1″ x 15″ piece into a loop; glue to secure. Place loops together and wrap remaining piece around centers of loops; glue to secure. For streamers, cut six 1″ x 7″ pieces from untwisted paper. Glue one end of each streamer to top center of egg. Notch remaining ends; glue notched ends to egg. Glue bow to streamers; arrange bow loops.
8. Glue greenery around bow and at center of bow. Glue flowers at center of bow.

# BUNNY TREAT
(Shown on page 34)

*You will need* orange and natural Paper Capers™ twisted paper, polyester fiberfill, dried plumosa fern, Design Master® glossy wood tone spray (available at craft stores), 8″ of florist wire, craft glue, hot glue gun, and glue sticks.

1. Cut three 10″ lengths and three 8″ lengths from untwisted orange paper.
2. Place a 1″ thick piece of fiberfill along center of one length of paper. Overlap long edges of paper over fiberfill, tapering at one end; cut away excess paper as needed (Fig. 1). Use craft glue to secure. Twist ½″ of narrow end together to form a point and fold remaining end 1″ to seam side of carrot; use craft glue to secure each end. Repeat for remaining lengths.

Fig. 1

3. (Note: Refer to photo for Steps 3 - 5.) Spray carrots with wood tone spray; allow to dry. Arrange carrots and hot glue together.
4. Hot glue pieces of fern at tops of carrots.
5. For bow, cut one 52″ length from untwisted natural paper; make a 7″ wide multi-loop bow with streamers. Hot glue bow to carrots.
6. For hanger, insert wire through top center at back of carrots; twist ends of wire together to form a loop.

# SPRINGTIME BOUQUET AND WREATH
(Shown on pages 31 and 33)

*You will need* silk flowers, gesso, white and desired colors of acrylic paint, flat paintbrushes, florist wire, wire cutters, and paper towels.
*For bouquet,* you will also need waxed paper and desired size bow made from craft ribbon.
*For wreath,* you will also need one grapevine wreath, brown crepe florist tape, hot glue gun, and glue sticks.

1. (Note: For flowers in bouquet, apply gesso and paint to blossoms, stems, and leaves. For flowers in wreath, apply gesso and paint to blossoms and leaves only.) Apply one coat of gesso to flowers; allow to dry. Paint flowers desired colors; allow to dry.
2. Use white paint to dry brush flowers. To dry brush, use a dry paintbrush and dip tips of bristles in paint. Brush tips across paper towels to remove excess paint. Lightly stroke brush across surface of each flower, highlighting prominent areas; allow to dry.
3. For bouquet, apply one coat of gesso to bow. Arrange bow on waxed paper and allow to dry. Apply two more coats of gesso to bow, allowing to dry between coats. Paint bow and allow to dry. Wire stems of flowers together to form bouquet; wire bow to bouquet.
4. For wreath, remove vines from wreath until two or three circles of vine remain. Cover wire with florist tape; use wire to secure vines. Referring to photo, glue blossoms and leaves to wreath.

# GRAPEVINE TREE (Shown on page 32)

*This tree is easiest to make in summer or early fall when fresh vines are plentiful. We used wild muscadine vines, but almost any type of vine can be used.*

*For a 21" tree,* you will need freshly cut vines, 20-gauge florist wire wrapped with brown crepe florist tape, work gloves, and wire cutters.

1. Allow vines to dry for one day after harvesting. Wearing gloves, strip all leaves from vines.

2. For base of tree, form several vines into an approximately 10" dia. circle. To secure, refer to Fig. 1 and wrap additional vines around circle.

Fig. 1

3. To form tree shape, cut several 24" lengths of sturdy straight vines. Insert large end of each vine into base as shown in Fig. 2. Add more straight vines as needed to get a full shape. Wire vines together at top of tree. Wire vines to base.

Fig. 2

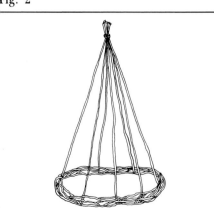

4. To fill in tree shape, use an in-and-out weaving motion to weave one vine around straight vines of tree shape (Fig. 3a). Continue weaving additional vines around straight vines until tree shape is filled in (Fig. 3b); tuck ends of vines into tree.

Fig. 3a

Fig. 3b

5. For looped vines, loosely loop vines around woven vines as shown in Fig. 4. Referring to photo, continue looping vines until desired shape is achieved; tuck ends of vines into tree. Use wire cutters to trim undesired vines.

Fig. 4

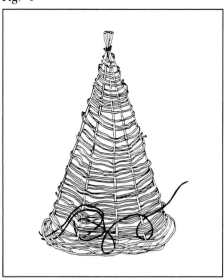

# SPONGED EGGS
(Shown on pages 32, 35, and 37)

*For each large egg,* you will need one 2" long plastic egg, newspaper, and craft glue.

*For each small egg,* you will need one 1" long plastic egg.

*You will also need* gesso, medium sandpaper, foam brushes, ivory and desired color acrylic paint, small piece of cellulose sponge, and a paper towel.

1. To prepare large egg, tear newspaper into approximately ⅜" x 2" strips. Follow Steps 2 - 4 of Antiqued Egg instructions, page 38.

2. To prepare small egg, lightly sand seams. Use a foam brush to apply two coats of gesso to egg, allowing to dry between coats.

3. Paint egg ivory; allow to dry.

4. Dampen sponge and squeeze out excess water. Dip sponge into desired color paint; blot excess on paper towel. Referring to photo and using an up-and-down stamping motion, apply a light coat of paint to egg; allow to dry.

# BUNNY COUPLE   (Shown on page 29)

*For boy bunny,* you will need natural, country blue, dk blue, orange, and white Paper Capers™ twisted paper; three 6″ lengths of ¹⁄₁₆″w brown satin ribbon; thread to match country blue paper; one ½″ dia. brown button; four ⅛″ dia. white buttons; Design Master® glossy wood tone spray (available at craft stores); and dried plumosa fern.

*For girl bunny,* you will need natural, pink, and white Paper Capers™ twisted paper; three 6″ lengths of ¹⁄₁₆″w cream satin ribbon; thread to match pink paper; one ½″ dia. pink button; two ⅛″ dia. white buttons; and a 3″ dia. twig basket filled with dried flowers.

*You will also need* two 9″ long plastic eggs with flat bases and clear, removable tops; 12″ x 18″ piece of heavy cardboard; two 3″ dia. plastic foam balls; 4 cups of dried beans; polyester fiberfill; craft glue; hot glue gun; glue sticks; wire cutters; and 18-gauge florist wire.

## BOY BUNNY

1. Place 2 cups of beans in one egg; hot glue egg halves together.

2. For base, cut one 5½″ dia. circle from cardboard. Center and hot glue base to large end of egg.

3. (Note: When using twisted paper, cut paper the specified length and untwist. Use entire width of paper unless stated otherwise.) For head, refer to Fig. 1a and flatten one foam ball to 2″ wide (flattened sides of ball will be sides of head). Cut four 14″ lengths of natural paper. Referring to Fig. 1b, wrap one length of paper around ball to cover sides of head; use another length to wrap around remainder of head. Use wire to secure paper at base of head. Repeat, using remaining lengths of paper.

Fig. 1a

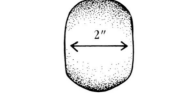

Fig. 1b

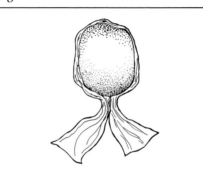

4. (Note: Flat area of egg is back of bunny.) Referring to Fig. 2, center and hot glue head to small end of egg.

Fig. 2

5. For each ear, cut one 16″ length of natural paper and one 6″ length of wire. With 2″ of wire extending beyond one short edge of paper, center wire on paper (Fig. 3a). Hot glue wire in place. Matching short edges, fold paper in half over wire. Twist short edges of paper together and use craft glue to secure (Fig. 3b); allow to dry.

Fig. 3a

Fig. 3b

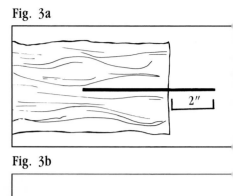

6. Apply craft glue to ear wires. Referring to photo, insert ear wires into head; allow to dry. Bend ears as desired.

7. For whiskers and nose, knot ends of each ribbon length. Referring to photo, hot glue centers of lengths to back of ½″ dia. button; hot glue button to head.

8. For body, cut two 28″ lengths of country blue paper. Overlapping long edges ¼″, use craft glue to glue pieces together to form a strip; allow to dry. Matching short edges, fold strip in half (folded edge is bottom). Using a ¼″ seam allowance, sew sides together to form a bag; turn right side out. Place egg, base first, into bag.

9. Gather bag around neck of bunny and secure with wire; trim excess paper. Fold bottom corners of bag under base of bunny; hot glue to secure.

10. For collar, cut a 1½″ x 5″ piece of white paper and fold in half lengthwise. Wrap paper around neck; use craft glue to secure.

1. For each foot, cut one ½″ x 2¼″ piece of cardboard; round off corners. For toes, hot glue a ″ dia. piece of fiberfill at one end of cardboard (Fig. 4). Cut a 9″ length of natural paper. Place cardboard, fiberfill side down, on paper and fold edges of paper around cardboard; hot glue to secure.

Fig. 4

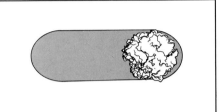

2. Referring to photo, hot glue feet to base.

3. For each hand, cut one 6″ length of natural paper. Center a cotton ball-sized piece of fiberfill on paper; overlap long edges of paper over fiberfill and use craft glue to secure. Matching short edges, fold paper in half and twist ends together (Fig. 5).

Fig. 5

4. For each arm, cut one 8″ length of country blue paper. Overlap long edges ¼″ to form a tube and use craft glue to secure. Fold one end of tube 1″ to seam side and use craft glue to secure (Fig. 6a); allow to dry. Stuff tube lightly with fiberfill. Insert twisted end of one hand into tube opening and use wire to secure (Fig. 6b). For each cuff, cut one ½″ x 3″ piece of white paper and fold in half lengthwise. Wrap paper over wire; use craft glue to secure.

Fig. 6a

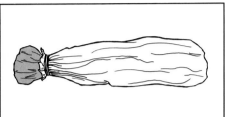

Fig. 6b

15. Referring to photo, hot glue tops of arms to body.

16. For tail, cut one 4″ length of white paper. Overlap short edges of paper ¼″ and use craft glue to secure. Pinch paper together along glued area and hot glue to back of bunny.

17. For belt and suspenders, cut three 20″ x 1″ pieces of dk blue paper and fold in half lengthwise. Referring to photo, use craft glue to secure; trim excess paper. Referring to photo, hot glue white buttons to body.

18. For bow tie, cut one 1½″ x 8½″ piece for bow and one ½″ x 1″ piece for center from dk blue paper. Overlap short edges of bow piece to form a loop. Wrap center piece around bow and use craft glue to secure. Hot glue bow to collar.

19. For each carrot, cut one 1″ x 2¾″ piece of orange paper. Center a 2″ long piece of fiberfill on paper. Overlap long edges of paper over fiberfill; use craft glue to secure. Twist one end together to form a point. Fold remaining end ½″ to seam side of carrot; use craft glue to secure each end (Fig. 7). Repeat to make three carrots. Spray carrots with wood tone spray.

Fig. 7

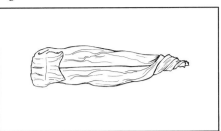

20. Referring to photo, hot glue carrots to bottom of hand. Hot glue small pieces of fern to top of hand. Hot glue hands to body.

GIRL BUNNY

1. For base, head, ears, whiskers, and nose, follow Steps 1 - 7 of Boy Bunny instructions, page 40.

2. For body, use pink paper and follow Step 8 of Boy Bunny instructions, page 40.

3. Gather bag around neck of bunny and secure with wire. Referring to photo, fold excess paper down over wire to form collar. Fold bottom corners of bag under base of bunny; hot glue to secure.

4. For feet, hands, arms, and tail, use pink paper for arms and follow Steps 11 - 16 of Boy Bunny instructions.

5. For apron, cut four 6″ lengths of white paper. Overlapping long edges ¼″, use craft glue to glue pieces together to form a strip.

6. For apron tie, cut one 1½″ x 18″ piece of white paper and fold in half lengthwise. On one side of apron tie, mark 4½″ from each short edge; apply a line of craft glue between marks. Glue one long edge of apron to apron tie, gathering apron edge to fit between marks; allow to dry.

7. Referring to photo, hot glue apron to bunny. Hot glue white buttons to body. Place basket on arm. Hot glue hands to body.

8. For bow, cut a ½″ x 14″ piece of pink paper and tie in a bow. Referring to photo, hot glue bow to ear.

## PAPER BUNNIES (Shown on pages 32, 33, 34, and 35)

*For each bunny ornament,* you will need one bunny candy mold (we used 3½", 4", and 4½"h plastic molds) and desired colors of 64 lb. charcoal drawing paper (for backing).

*For standing bunny,* you will need one two-sided bunny candy mold (we used a 7"h metal candy mold); small, sharp scissors; polyester fiberfill; lightweight cardboard (for bottom of bunny); ⅛"w satin ribbon; and dried greenery.

*For framed bunny,* you will need one bunny cookie mold (we used a 4½"h ceramic cookie mold), desired color of 64 lb. charcoal drawing paper (for backing), desired color mat board (for mounting), and desired frame (we used a custom frame).

*You will also need* 140 lb., ph neutral, watercolor paper; a 13 x 9 x 2-inch pan; wooden meat mallet; several cellulose sponges; small spray bottle filled with diluted coffee (two parts water to one part coffee); diluted acrylic paints (two parts water to one part paint); #6 flat paintbrush; #00 liner paintbrush; craft glue; desired dried flowers; and matte clear acrylic spray.

### BUNNY ORNAMENT

1. Tear a piece of watercolor paper 2" larger on all sides than mold. Place paper in pan and cover with boiling water. Use a spoon to push down corners of paper as it curls. Let paper soak at least three hours.
2. Cut sponges into approximately 1½" long wedge-shaped pieces.
3. Place paper on a hard, flat, non-absorbent surface. Keeping paper wet, use mallet to lightly pound each side of paper for approximately one minute. Repeat until paper is soft and pliable and the mallet leaves deep indentations in the paper.
4. Carefully press paper into mold using fingers and dry sponge wedges to push paper into mold details and to remove excess water. (If paper springs back out of mold, return paper to work surface and continue pounding process for several more minutes.) Continue pressing paper into mold until paper fills all mold indentations and most of water is removed. If paper tears, patch with a small piece of soaked paper.
5. Without pulling paper out of mold, carefully tear excess paper approximately ¼" from edges of mold and discard. Use dry sponge wedges to press paper into mold once more.
6. Allow paper to dry in mold for several hours. When paper is completely dry, remove from mold.
7. Spray bunny with diluted coffee until damp but not saturated.
8. (Note: Refer to photo, page 32, for Steps 8 - 10. All painting should be done while bunny is damp; spray with diluted coffee as needed.) Using diluted paints and flat paintbrush, paint base coat on bunny. Highlight raised areas with a lighter color. Use liner paintbrush and a darker color to shade creases and to paint details. Allow to dry.
9. For backing, cut a piece of charcoal paper 1" larger than bunny on all sides. Glue edges of bunny to charcoal paper; allow to dry. Tear excess backing paper approximately ¼" from torn edges of bunny and discard. Repeat if desired for second layer of backing paper.
10. Glue flowers to bunny. Spray with two light coats of acrylic spray, allowing to dry between coats.

### STANDING BUNNY

1. To make each bunny piece, follow Steps 1 - 4 of Bunny Ornament instructions. To quickly dry paper in a metal mold, place mold on a cookie sheet in a preheated 350 degree oven; turn oven off. Paper will dry in approximately 30 minutes.
2. To paint bunny pieces, refer to photo, page 35, and follow Steps 7 and 8 of Bunny Ornament instructions.
3. Use scissors to carefully trim excess paper from each bunny piece.
4. For tabs to connect bunny pieces, cut ¼" x ½" pieces from dry watercolor paper. Matching short edges, fold each tab in half. Refer to Fig. 1 and glue one end of each tab to inside edge of one bunny piece; allow to dry. Beginning at front of bunny piece and matching edges, glue remaining end of each tab inside edge of remaining bunny piece; allow to dry

Fig. 1

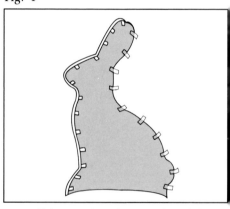

5. Stuff bunny lightly with fiberfill.
6. Set bunny on cardboard and draw around base; cut out shape from cardboard. Place cardboard slightly inside opening at base of bunny, trimming to fit; glue in place.
7. Spray with two light coats of acrylic spray, allowing to dry between coats. Referring to photo, tie ribbon in a bow around neck; trim streamers and glue in place. Glue greenery and flowers to bunny.

### FRAMED BUNNY

1. To make bunny, refer to photo, page 33, and follow Bunny Ornament instructions.
2. Glue bunny to mat board.
3. Frame as desired.

# BOOKMARK (Shown on page 30)

*Finished Size:* Approximately 2" x 6"

## ABBREVIATIONS

| | |
|---|---|
| ch(s) | chain(s) |
| dc | double crochet(s) |
| sl st | slip stitch |
| st(s) | stitch(es) |

) or [ ] — work enclosed instructions *as many* times as specified by the number immediately following *or* contains explanatory remarks.

## MATERIALS

DMC Cebelia Art. 167/size 30, ecru - one ball (approximately 563 yards)

Steel crochet hook, size 10 (1.15 mm) *or* size needed for gauge

Purchased tassel with hanging loop

## GAUGE

22 dc and 8 rows = 1"
DO NOT HESITATE TO CHANGE HOOK SIZE TO OBTAIN CORRECT GAUGE.

## WORKING WITH CHARTS

Each blank square on the chart represents one Space (ch 2, dc) and each grey square represents one Block (3 dc). For right side rows, the chart should be read from right to left; for wrong side rows, the chart should be read from left to right.

## INSTRUCTIONS

Ch 48 *loosely.*

*Row 1:* Dc in 4th ch from hook and in next 44 chs.

*Row 2:* [Ch 3, turn, dc in next 3 dc *(beginning Block over Block made)*], [ch 2, skip 2 dc, dc in next dc *(Space over Block made)*] 13 times, [dc in next 3 dc *(Block over Block made)*].

*Row 3:* Work beginning Block, [ch 2, dc in next dc *(Space over Space made)*], [work 2 dc in next Space, dc in next dc *(Block over Space made)*], follow chart across.

*Rows 4 - 43:* Follow chart.

*Row 44:* [Turn, sl st in first 4 dc, ch 3 *(beginning decrease made)*], follow chart across, leaving last 3 sts unworked.

*Rows 45 - 48:* Follow chart, finish off.

## FINISHING

Using crochet hook, draw hanging loop of tassel through top center stitch of Bookmark; insert tassel through loop and pull to draw loop up tightly.

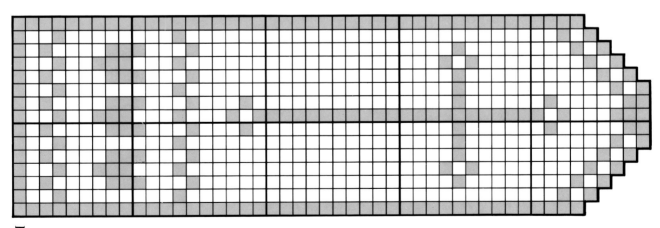

Row 1

43

# EASTER LAMBS (Shown on pages 30 and 31)

*For each large lamb,* you will need one 4″ and one 5″ long plastic foam egg and one 2″ dia. plastic foam ball. *For each small lamb,* you will need one 2½″ and one 3″ long plastic foam egg and one 1½″ dia. plastic foam ball.

*You will also need* instant papier mâché (one 1 lb. package will make three large lambs), toothpicks, gesso, black acrylic paint, matte clear acrylic spray, foam brushes, flat paintbrush, craft glue, utility knife, a soft cloth, resealable plastic bag, walnut water-based stain, blue and green Paper Capers™ twisted paper, matte white spray paint, and small pink ribbon roses.

Note: Instructions are written for the large lamb with sizes for the small lamb in parentheses.

1. Use utility knife to cut foam ball in half.
2. Break one toothpick in half. Coat toothpick halves and one whole toothpick with glue. Referring to Fig. 1, use toothpicks to assemble foam pieces.

Fig. 1

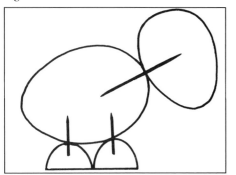

3. Referring to photo, position lamb's head.
4. Following manufacturer's instructions, mix papier mâché. Store mixture in resealable plastic bag. (Papier mâché will keep for several days in the refrigerator.)

5. Use a foam brush to apply glue around neck and tops of legs. Referring to Fig. 2, apply papier mâché over glued areas. Allow papier mâché to dry overnight or until hard and dry.

Fig. 2

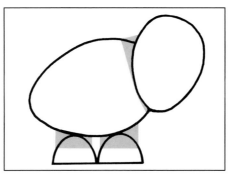

6. Place a small amount of papier mâché in a small bowl and add water until mixture is very soft. Referring to grey areas in Fig. 3, use foam brush to apply glue to head and legs. Smooth papier mâché mixture over glued areas; allow to dry.

Fig. 3

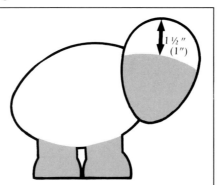

7. Apply glue to a small section of body. Using regular papier mâché mixture, apply small pieces to glued area. Repeat to cover remaining foam on head and body.
8. Referring to grey area in Fig. 4, apply glue around face. Apply small pieces of papier mâché to glued area.

Fig. 4

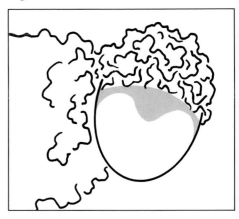

9. For tail and ears, form three ⅜″ dia. rolls 2¾″ (1″) long from papier mâché. Flatten each roll slightly. Press one end of one roll onto back of lamb for tail. Use fingernail to make a crease along center of each remaining roll. Referring to photo, press one end of each roll onto head to form ears; allow to dry.
10. Apply two coats of gesso to lamb, allowing to dry between coats.
11. Referring to photo, use flat paintbrush to paint face and legs black; allow to dry.
12. Apply stain to lamb and remove excess with soft cloth; allow to dry.
13. Spray lamb with acrylic spray.
14. Lightly spray untwisted paper and roses with spray paint. For bow, cut blue paper desired length and width. Referring to photo, place paper around neck and form into a bow; glue in place. Cut leaf-shaped pieces from green paper. Glue leaves and roses to bow.

# SWEETHEARTS  (Shown on page 36)

*You will need* one 9" x 11" piece of Cream Belfast Linen (32 ct), embroidery floss (see color key), embroidery hoop (optional), and desired frame (we used a custom frame).

1. Follow Working On Linen, page 125, to work design over two fabric threads. Use 2 strands of floss for Cross Stitch, 1 for Backstitch, and 1 for French Knots.
2. Frame as desired.

## SWEETHEARTS  (55w x 78h)

| X | DMC | ¼X | B'ST | ANC. | COLOR |
|---|-----|----|----|------|-------|
| | ecru | | | 0387 | ecru |
| | 315 | | | 0896 | purple |
| | 316 | | | 0969 | lt purple |
| | 347 | | | 020 | red |
| | 433 | | | 0371 | brown |
| | 435 | | | 0365 | lt brown |
| | 437 | | | 0362 | tan |
| | 500 | | | 0879 | vy dk blue green |
| | 501 | | | 0878 | dk blue green |
| | 502 | | | 0876 | blue green |
| | 503 | | | 0875 | lt blue green |
| | 676 | | | 0891 | yellow |
| | 760 | | | 08 | pink |
| | 930 | | | 0922 | dk blue |
| | 931 | | | 0921 | blue |
| | 932 | | | 0920 | lt blue |
| | 938 | | | 0381 | dk brown |
| | 986 | | | 0246 | green |
| | 3078 | | | 0292 | lt yellow |
| | 3328 | | | 010 | lt red |
| | 3347 | | | 0266 | lt green |
| | 938 | | | | dk brown French Knot |

| SWEETHEARTS (55w x 78h) | | |
|---|---|---|
| Aida 11 | 5" | x 7⅛" |
| Aida 14 | 4" | x 5⅝" |
| Aida 18 | 3⅛" | x 4⅜" |
| Hardanger 22 | 2½" | x 3⅝" |

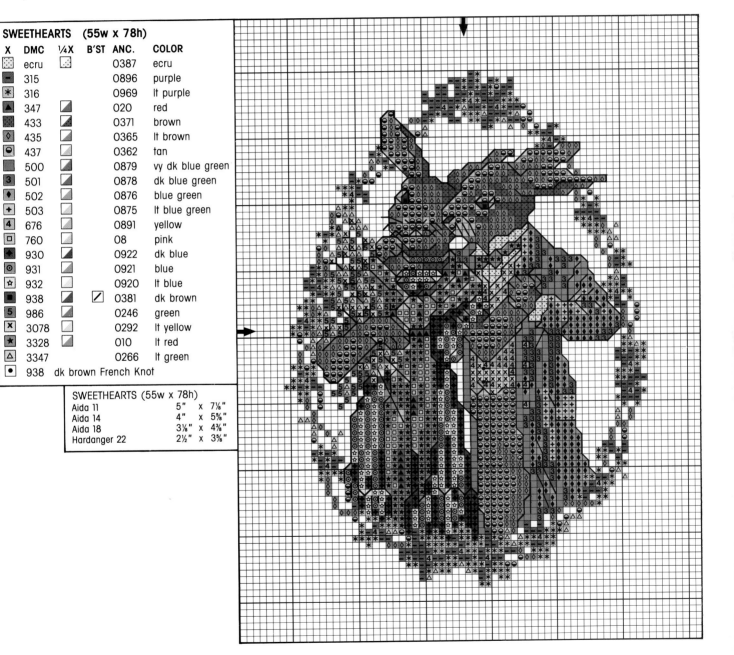

# Mother's Day
# Father's Day

*Mother's Day and Father's Day
are times for saying ''I love you'' to
the people who have nurtured us
from the moment we took our first
breaths. These special days bestow
golden opportunities to recount tender
memories of a family's beginnings.
Coupled with precious mementos, the
stories recalled by our parents reveal
their enduring love and strengthen
our spirit of togetherness. When we
craft tokens of affection to honor
those who made us a family,
we create heirlooms for
coming generations.*

Instructions for this collection begin on page 50.

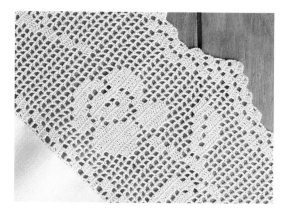

*S*weet reminders of the past are assurances
that bygone days will not be forgotten. Presented on
Father's Day, a collage of childhood pictures, carefully
preserved on an album box, recalls the carefree days
of youth and the special bond shared when you were
Daddy's little girl. And what sweeter Mother's Day gift
could you offer than a handcrafted frame to hold a
cherished photograph of her mother. With these thoughtful
tokens, we embrace memories that will last forever.

## PADDED FRAME  (Shown on page 49)

*You will need* ⅔ yd of 44″w fabric, ¾ yd of ⅛″ dia. cord, lightweight fusible interfacing, mat board or heavy cardboard, fabric marking pencil, utility knife, craft batting, tracing paper, craft glue, spring-type clothespins, and 24″ of ⅜″w grosgrain ribbon.

1. For frame pattern, fold a 9″ square of tracing paper in half from top to bottom and again left to right. Placing folds of paper along dashed lines of pattern, trace pattern; cut out. Unfold pattern. For easel pattern, follow Transferring Patterns, page 124.
2. For frame front, use frame pattern and cut one piece from mat board and batting. For frame back, omit opening from frame pattern and cut one piece from mat board. For easel, use easel pattern and cut one piece from mat board.
3. Cut two 11″ fabric squares for frame front and back and one 7″ x 8″ fabric piece for easel. Cut interfacing slightly smaller than fabric pieces. Following manufacturer's instructions, fuse interfacing to wrong sides of fabric pieces.
4. For frame front, center board (with opening) on wrong side of one fabric square. Cut fabric 1″ larger than board on all sides. Use fabric marking pencil to draw around opening. Draw another line 1″ inside pencil line (Fig. 1). Set board aside. Cut opening on inside line. At ½″ intervals, clip fabric to within ⅛″ of first pencil line (Fig. 2).

Fig. 1

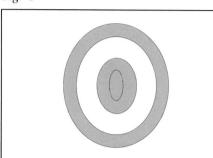

Fig. 2

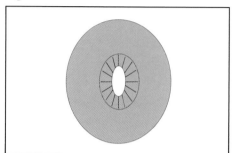

5. Glue batting to one side of frame front board. Place board, batting side down, on wrong side of fabric. Alternating sides, glue clipped edges of fabric to back of board. Allow to dry.
6. At ½″ intervals, clip fabric to within ⅛″ of outer edge of board. Alternating sides and pulling fabric tightly around board, glue clipped edges of fabric to back of board. Allow to dry.
7. For cording, cut one 1½″ x 24″ bias strip. Lay cord along center on wrong side of bias strip. Matching long edges, fold strip over cord. Use zipper foot and machine baste along length of strip close to cord. Trim seam allowance to ½″. Referring to photo, glue cording around frame front; overlap ends and trim excess. Glue ends to wrong side of board.
8. For frame back, center board on wrong side of remaining fabric square. Cut fabric 1″ larger than board on all sides and follow Step 6 to cover board with fabric. Cut a piece of fabric ⅛″ smaller on all sides than board. With wrong sides together, glue fabric to board (this will be the wrong side of frame back).
9. With wrong sides together and leaving top open to insert picture, glue front to back; secure with clothespins. Remove clothespins before glue completely dries.
10. For easel, center board on wrong side of fabric. Fold fabric to back of board, overlapping edges and trimming as necessary; glue to secure. Fold easel on right side where indicated on pattern by dotted lines. With bottom edges even, center wrong side of easel on back of frame; glue area above dotted line to frame.
11. Referring to photo, tie ribbon in a bow and glue to front of frame.

Fold line

EASEL    FRAME

# FILET EDGING (Shown on pages 47 and 48)

*Finished size:* Approximately 4″ wide

## ABBREVIATIONS

ch(s)   chain(s)
dc      double crochet(s)
sl st   slip stitch
st(s)   stitch(es)
YO      yarn over

( ) or [ ] — work enclosed
    instructions *as many* times as
    specified by the number
    immediately following *or*
    contains explanatory remarks.

## MATERIALS

DMC Cebelia Art. 167/size 30,
    ecru - one ball
    (approximately 563 yards)
Steel crochet hook, size 10
    (1.15 mm) *or* size needed for
    gauge

GAUGE: 22 dc and 8 rows = 1″
    DO NOT HESITATE TO
    CHANGE HOOK SIZE TO
    OBTAIN CORRECT GAUGE.

## WORKING WITH CHARTS

Each blank square on the chart
represents one Space (ch 2, dc) and
each grey square represents one Block
(3 dc). For right side rows, the chart
should be read from right to left; for
wrong side rows, the chart should be
read from left to right.

## INSTRUCTIONS

Ch 90 *loosely.*

*Row 1* (Right side): Dc in 4th ch from
hook and in next 2 chs, ch 2, skip
2 chs, dc in next 4 chs, (ch 2, skip
2 chs, dc in next ch) 11 times, dc in
next 3 chs, (ch 2, skip 2 chs, dc in
next ch) 13 times, dc in last 3 chs.

*Row 2:* [Ch 3, turn, dc in next 3 dc
*(beginning Block over Block made)*],
[ch 2, dc in next dc *(Space over Space
made)*] 13 times, [dc in next 3 dc
*(Block over Block made)*], work
10 Spaces, [work 2 dc in next Space,
dc in next dc *(Block over Space
made)*], [ch 2, skip 2 dc, dc in next
dc *(Space over Block made)*], work
Block, leave last 3 sts unworked.

*Row 3:* Follow chart.

*Row 4:* [Ch 5, turn, dc in next dc
*(beginning Space over Space made)*],
follow chart across.

*Row 5:* Follow chart across to last
Space, work 3 dc.

*Rows 6 - 8:* Follow chart.

*Row 9:* [Turn, sl st in first 4 dc, ch 3
*(beginning decrease made)*], follow
chart across.

*Rows 10 - 11:* Follow chart.

*Row 12:* Follow chart across, work
end increase as follows: [YO, insert
hook into base of last dc and pull up
a loop, YO and draw through one
loop on hook, (YO and draw through
2 loops on hook) twice] 3 times.

*Rows 13 - 14:* Follow chart.

*Row 15:* [Ch 5, turn, dc in 4th ch
from hook and in next ch, dc in next
dc *(beginning increase made)*], follow
chart across.

*Rows 16 - 76:* Follow chart.
Repeat Rows 1 - 76 until edging is
desired length; finish off.

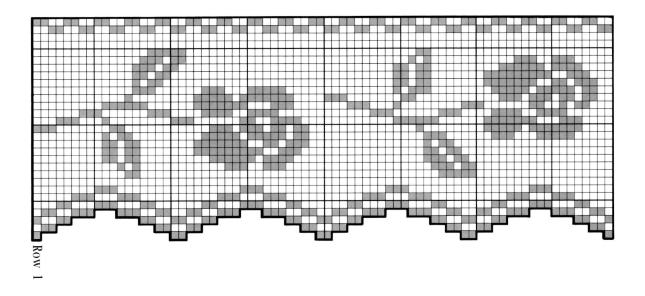

Row 1

51

# ALBUM BOX
(Shown on page 48)

*You will need* one wooden box, burgundy acrylic paint, photocopies of old photographs, Design Master® glossy wood tone spray (available at craft stores), black photo mounting corners, craft glue, metallic gold paint marker with fine point, matte Mod Podge™ sealer, medium walnut water-based stain, #400 wet/dry sandpaper, paintbrushes, and a soft cloth.

1. Paint box; allow to dry.
2. Lightly spray photocopies with wood tone spray. Glue photo mounting corners to some of the photocopies.
3. Refer to photo and use a pencil to lightly write message and draw border on box. Draw over pencil lines with paint marker; allow to dry.
4. Arrange photos on box lid as desired. Use sealer to glue photos to box lid; allow to dry.
5. Apply stain to entire project and remove excess with soft cloth; allow to dry.
6. Apply five coats of sealer to box, allowing to dry between coats.
7. Use sandpaper to wet-sand box, smoothing any ridges or bubbles.

# SAMPLER
(Shown on page 47)

*You will need* one 14" x 17" piece of Cream Lugana (25 ct), embroidery floss (see color key), embroidery hoop (optional), and desired frame (we used a custom frame).

1. Work design over two fabric threads, using 3 strands of floss for Cross Stitch, 1 for Backstitch, and 1 for French Knots. Use alphabet and numbers at top of chart to personalize sampler.
2. Frame as desired.

## SAMPLER (95w x 130h)

| X | DMC | 1/4X | B'ST | ANC. | COLOR |
|---|-----|------|------|------|-------|
| | 434 | | | 0310 | dk gold |
| | 435 | | | 0365 | gold |
| | 437 | | | 0362 | lt gold |
| | 500 | | | 0879 | vy dk green |
| | 501 | | | 0878 | dk green |
| | 502 | | | 0876 | green |
| | 503 | | | 0875 | lt green |
| | 738 | | | 0361 | vy lt green |

| X | DMC | 1/4X | B'ST | ANC. | COLOR |
|---|-----|------|------|------|-------|
| | 930 | | | 0922 | dk blue French Knot |
| | 931 | | | 0921 | blue |
| | 3685 | | | 065 | dk rose |
| | 3687 | | | 077 | rose |
| | 3688 | | | 076 | lt rose |

Grey area indicates last row of top section of design.

| SAMPLER (95w x 130h) | |
|---|---|
| Aida 11 | 8¾" x 11⅞" |
| Aida 14 | 6⅞" x 9⅜" |
| Aida 18 | 5⅜" x 7¼" |
| Hardanger 22 | 4⅜" x 6" |

52

# PATRIOTIC DAYS

*Celebrating a star-spangled Fourth
of July; unfurling Old Glory on Flag
Day, Memorial Day, or Veterans Day;
honoring our distinguished leaders
on Presidents' Day — all these
things inspire us to say,
''I'm proud to be an American.''
With our national colors and symbols
boldly displayed, reminders of
our freedoms and privileges abound,
making patriotic occasions some of
the most spirited days of the year.*

Instructions for this collection begin on page 60.

P resented in rustic fashion, stars and stripes help us recall the grass roots culture of our great land. Hearkening back to our ancestors' creative ingenuity, carved soap stars reflect the high aspirations of our founding fathers.

*erbaps nothing brings to mind more the proud heritage of America than our national colors. Quilted from old-fashioned fabrics, a flag-inspired wall hanging salutes the rich legacy passed down to us by great presidents like George Washington and Abraham Lincoln. And since the late 1800's, zealous Republicans and Democrats have declared their party affiliations with elephants and donkeys, mascots introduced by political cartoonist Thomas Nast.*

*He serves his party best*
*who serves the country best.*
— PRESIDENT RUTHERFORD B. HAYES

# PRESIDENTIAL SILHOUETTES  (Shown on pages 57 and 59)

*For each silhouette,* you will need one 4" x 6" piece of black silhouette paper; tracing paper; graphite transfer paper; small, sharp scissors; one 14" x 9" piece of medium weight cardboard; one 14" x 9" piece of craft batting; 2 yds of 1½"w black grosgrain ribbon; 30" of ⅝"w black grosgrain ribbon; black felt-tip marker; removable tape; rubber cement; hot glue gun; glue sticks; photocopy of a historical document; and Design Master® glossy wood tone spray (available at craft stores).

1. Trace silhouette pattern onto tracing paper. Use transfer paper to transfer silhouette pattern to wrong side (white side) of silhouette paper. Cut out silhouette. Use felt-tip marker to cover white edges of silhouette.

2. For frame pattern, fold one 9" square of tracing paper in half from top to bottom and again from left to right. Placing folds of paper along dashed lines of frame pattern on this page, trace pattern; cut out. Unfold pattern.

3. For frame front, use frame pattern and cut one piece from cardboard and two pieces from batting; hot glue both pieces of batting to one side (front) of cardboard. For frame back, omit opening from frame pattern and cut one piece from cardboard.

4. Referring to Fig. 1a, tape one end of 1½" wide ribbon to back of cardboard frame; overlapping edges, wrap ribbon around frame to within 1" of taped end. To complete wrapping, remove tape from wrapped end of ribbon; refer to Fig. 1b to tuck edge of free end of ribbon (trim end if necessary) under edge of previously wrapped ribbon. Hot glue ends to back of frame (Fig. 1c).

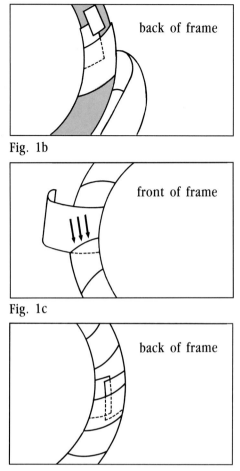

Fig. 1a

back of frame

Fig. 1b

front of frame

Fig. 1c

back of frame

5. Lightly spray photocopy with wood tone spray; allow to dry. Using frame back as a pattern, cut out photocopy. Use rubber cement to glue photocopy to frame back; allow to dry. Hot glue frame back to wrong side of frame front. Center silhouette in frame and use rubber cement to glue in place; allow to dry.

6. For hanger, refer to photo and use ⅝" wide ribbon to make a 4" wide double-loop bow with 4" long streamers. Hot glue ends of streamers to top back of frame.

# QUILTED FLAG BANNER (Shown on page 58)

*You will need* scraps of red and blue cotton fabric at least 2" x 12", one 18" square of red and white striped cotton fabric, one 8" square of navy cotton fabric, two 6" squares of fabric for star, 1 yd of 44"w fabric for binding, polyester fiberfill, thread to match fabric, quilting thread, tracing paper, white embroidery floss, paper-backed fusible web, one 14" x 28" piece of low-loft polyester bonded batting, one 14" x 28" piece of cotton fabric for backing, prepared instant coffee in a spray bottle, removable fabric marking pen, white fabric marking pencil, quilting hoop, quilting needle, 14" long twig, and 3-ply jute.

Note: For each sewing step, pin fabric pieces right sides together, matching raw edges; use a ¼" seam allowance throughout. Press all seam allowances away from center.

1. Wash, dry, and press all fabrics. Trim selvages from fabrics.

2. For flags, cut three 5½" x 7½" pieces of striped fabric with stripes running lengthwise, three 2¾" x 3½" pieces of navy fabric, and three 2½" x 3¼" pieces of fusible web. With one long edge at top, press right and bottom edges of each navy piece ¼" to wrong side. Referring to photo and matching raw edges, use fusible web and follow manufacturer's instructions to fuse one navy piece to each striped piece.

3. For strips, cut red and blue fabrics into 1½" wide strips.

4. (Note: Refer to Diagram for Steps 4 - 8.) To prepare strips 1, 2, 5, and 6, match one short edge of one blue and one red strip; sew short edges together. Press seam allowance to one side. Repeat to make a total of four strips.

5. For strip 1, align strip at left edge of flag with seam even with lower edge of navy piece; cut strip the width of the flag. Sew strip to left edge.

6. For strip 2, align strip at top edge of flag with seam even with right edge of navy piece; cut strip the length of flag plus attached strip. Sew strip to top edge.

7. For strip 3, cut one red strip the width of the flag plus attached strip. Sew strip to right edge.

8. Referring to Diagram for sewing order and color placement, continue attaching strips to complete one block.

9. Repeat Steps 4 - 8 to complete three quilt blocks.

10. For stars on flags, trace circular star placement pattern onto tracing paper and cut out. Referring to photo, center pattern on each navy piece and mark placement of each star with white pencil. Use 6 strands of floss and work one French Knot, page 125, at each mark.

11. Referring to Diagram, use fabric marking pen to draw four lines 1" apart across each flag.

12. For quilt top, refer to photo and sew quilt blocks together.

13. Cut backing fabric and batting 1" larger on all sides than quilt top. Place batting on wrong side of backing. Center quilt top, right side up, on batting. Smoothing any wrinkles in the quilt top, pin all layers together. Baste layers together from corner to corner and from side to side; remove pins.

14. (Note: For quilting lines on each block, refer to dashed lines on Diagram.) Insert basted layers in hoop, pulling materials taut. Begin quilting in the center, then work clockwise toward the edges of the quilt. Use quilting thread and Quilting Stitch, page 126, to quilt close to seamlines and along pen lines.

15. Trim batting and backing even with quilt top. Remove basting threads and pen marks.

16. For binding, cut one 1½" x 80" bias strip from binding fabric (piece as necessary). Follow Applying Binding, page 126, to finish edges of quilt.

17. Spray quilt and 6" fabric squares with coffee; allow to dry.

18. Whipstitch twig to top back of quilt.

19. For star, follow Transferring Patterns and Sewing Shapes, page 124, to make one star from fabric squares. Stuff star with fiberfill and sew final closure by hand.

20. For hanger, cut one 18" length of jute. Referring to photo, tie ends of jute to twig; whipstitch jute to center back of star.

**DIAGRAM KEY**
- ■ navy
- ■ red
- □ blue

**DIAGRAM**

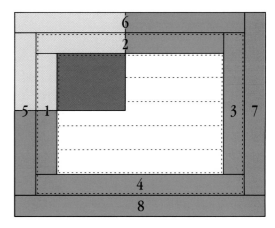

# STARS AND STRIPES TREE  (Shown on page 56)

## TREE
*You will need* freshly cut vines (see note in Grapevine Tree instructions, page 39), 20-gauge florist wire wrapped with brown crepe florist tape, work gloves, wire cutters, and desired container for base.

1. Making a 13″ dia. base and cutting 15″ long straight vines to form tree shape, follow Steps 1 - 4 of Grapevine Tree instructions, page 39.
2. To form wire base inside tree, refer to Fig. 1 and secure wires inside tree 1″ from bottom. Set tree on container.

Fig. 1

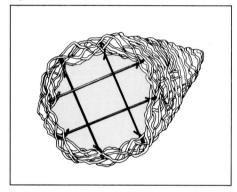

## SOAP STARS
*You will need* personal size bars of Ivory™ soap, 2″w star cookie cutter, and a sharp knife.

1. Cutting along length of soap, slowly slice each bar of soap into approximately ¼″ thick pieces.
2. Slowly press cookie cutter into one piece of soap. Remove soap star from cutter. Repeat for desired number of stars.

## FLAGS
*You will need* red and white striped fabric, scraps of denim fabric, paper-backed fusible web, toothpick, white acrylic paint, and spray bottle filled with strong instant coffee (2 tablespoons coffee to 1 cup water).

1. With stripes running lengthwise, tear striped fabric into approximately 2¼″ x 3″ pieces. Cut denim into approximately 1″ x 1½″ pieces; fringe edges of denim ⅛″.
2. Cut fusible web slightly smaller than denim pieces. Referring to photo, follow manufacturer's instructions to fuse denim pieces to striped pieces.
3. For stars on each flag, refer to photo and use toothpick dipped in paint to paint thirteen dots; allow to dry.
4. Spray flags with coffee; allow to dry.

## DECORATING THE TREE
*You will also need* red Paper Capers™ twisted paper, ½″ red and gold gummed stars, hot glue gun, and glue sticks.

1. Referring to photo, glue soap stars, flags, and gummed stars to tree.
2. For bow, cut a 2½″ x 40″ piece from untwisted paper; form into a 5″ wide bow with 12″ long streamers. Referring to photo, glue bow and streamers to tree.

# DEMOCRATIC DONKEY  (Shown on page 55)

*You will need* ⅓ yd of 44″w blue ticking fabric, two ½″ dia. and four ⅝″ dia. red buttons, polyester fiberfill, 3-ply jute, blue thread and thread to match fabric and jute, soft sculpture needle, instant coffee, tracing paper, fabric marking pencil, and small crochet hook (to turn fabric).

1. Dissolve 2 tablespoons instant coffee in 2 cups hot water; allow to cool. Soak fabric in coffee several minutes. Remove from coffee and allow to dry; press.
2. Cut eight 5″ x 7″ pieces of fabric for legs, two 7½″ x 10″ pieces of fabric for body, and four 4″ x 5½″ pieces of fabric for ears. Use donkey patterns, page 63, and follow Transferring Patterns and Sewing Shapes, page 124, to make four legs, one body, and two ears from fabric pieces. Stuff legs and body with fiberfill. Do not stuff ears. Leaving tail opening unstitched, sew final closures by hand.
3. Thread soft sculpture needle with a double strand of blue thread and securely knot ends together. For eyes, refer to photo and pattern and insert needle through body at ☆. Thread needle through one ½″ dia. button and insert needle back through body. Thread needle through remaining ½″ dia. button and insert needle back through body. Repeat to make several more stitches through buttons and body. Secure and clip thread.
4. Thread soft sculpture needle with a double strand of blue thread and securely knot ends together. To attach front legs to body, refer to photo and patterns and insert needle through one leg at **x**, through body at **x**, and through a second leg at **x**. Pull thread until legs are tight against

body. Thread needle through one
⅝" dia. button and insert needle back
through legs and body. Thread needle
through a second button and insert
needle back through legs and body.
Repeat to make several more stitches
through buttons, legs, and body.
Secure and clip thread. Repeat to
attach remaining legs to body.

5. Referring to photo, fold one ear in
half lengthwise; whipstitch to side of
head. Repeat to attach remaining ear.

6. For mane, cut one 8" length and
approximately twenty-five 5" lengths
of jute. Tie a knot 1" from one end of
8" length. Referring to Fig. 1, knot 5"
lengths of jute around 8" length. Knot
remaining end of 8" length close to 5"
lengths and trim 1" from knot.
Referring to pattern, whipstitch mane
to head at seamline between • • •'s.
Trim mane to 1" long.

Fig. 1

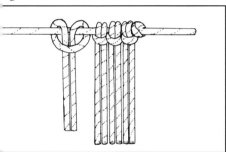

7. For tail, cut three 10" lengths of
jute. Knot lengths together 1" from
one end. Braid 3" and knot again.
Trim ends 1" from knot. Insert one
knotted end of jute into tail opening;
whipstitch opening closed around jute.

8. Untwist ends of jute in mane and
tail; use a straight pin to separate jute.

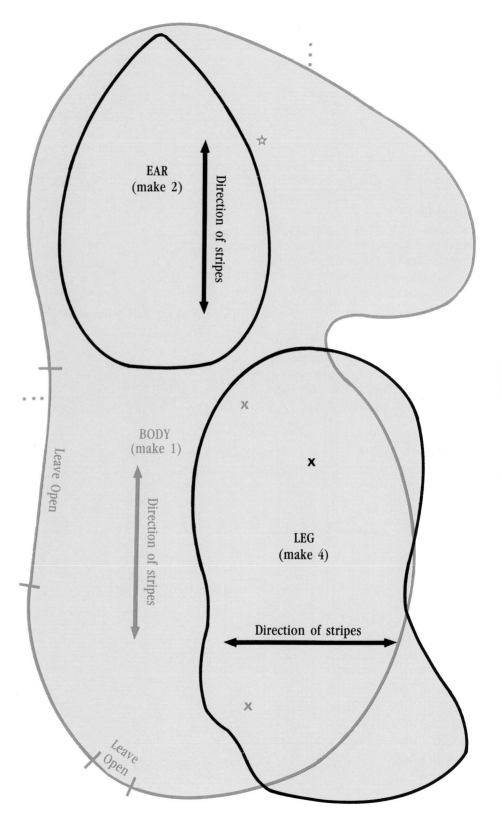

# REPUBLICAN ELEPHANT  (Shown on page 55)

*You will need* ⅓ yd of 44"w red ticking fabric, two ½" dia. and four ⅝" dia. blue buttons, polyester fiberfill, 3-ply jute, red thread and thread to match fabric, soft sculpture needle, instant coffee, tracing paper, fabric marking pencil, and small crochet hook (to turn fabric).

1. Use elephant patterns and follow Steps 1 - 4 of Democratic Donkey instructions, pages 62 and 63, to assemble elephant; use red thread to attach buttons.

2. Referring to photo, whipstitch one ear to each side of head.

3. For tail, cut three 8" lengths of jute. Knot lengths together 1" from one end. Braid 2" and knot again. Trim ends 1" from knot. Insert one knotted end of jute into tail opening; whipstitch opening closed around jute.

4. Untwist ends of jute in tail; use a straight pin to separate jute.

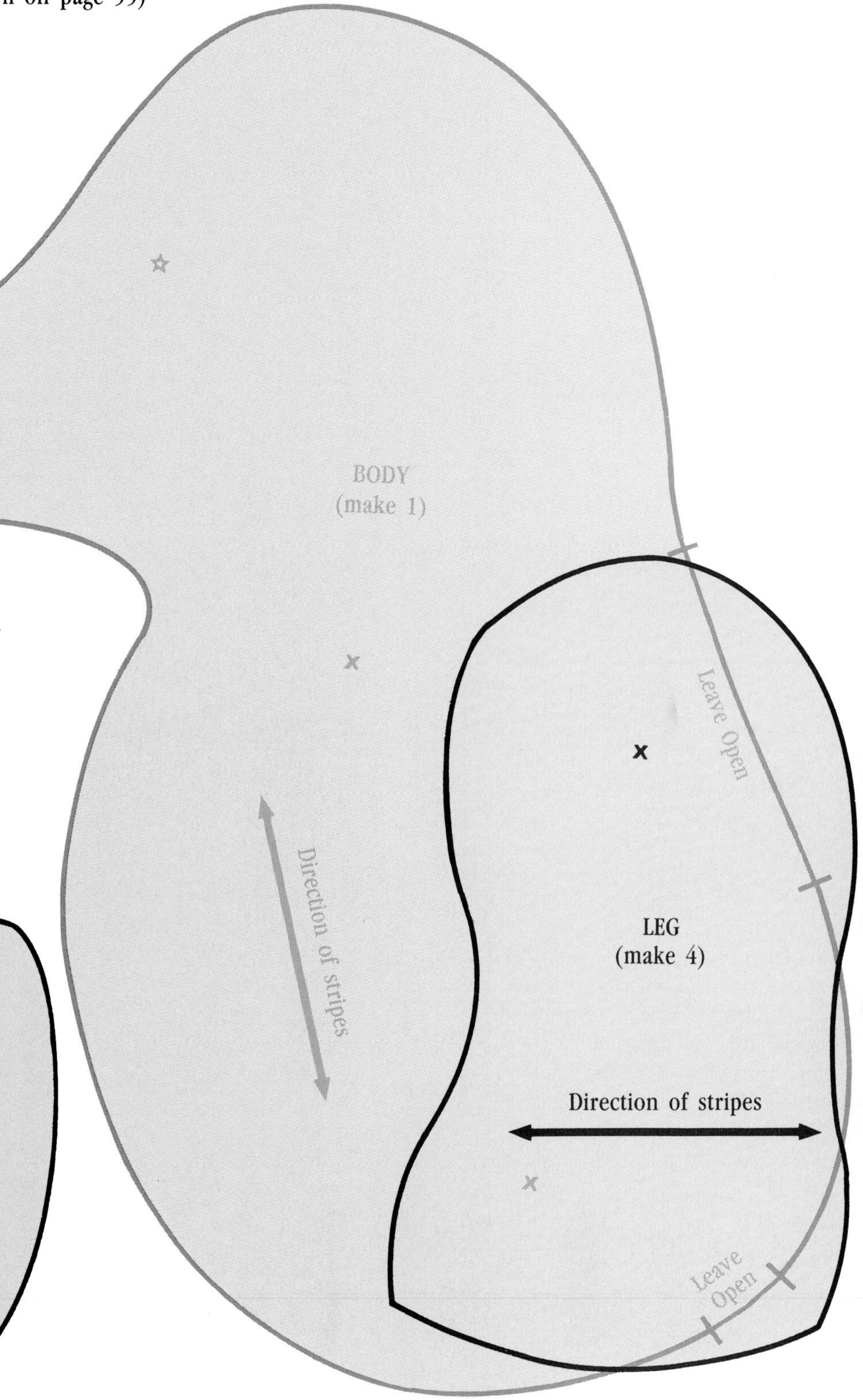

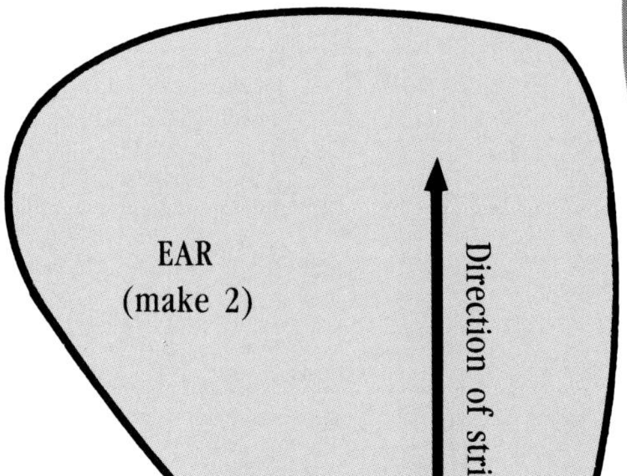

BODY
(make 1)

Direction of stripes

LEG
(make 4)

Leave Open

Leave Open

Direction of stripes

EAR
(make 2)

Direction of stripes

# PATRIOTIC STRING (Shown on page 59)

*You will need* four 8" squares of desired fabric for donkeys and four 8" squares of desired fabric for elephants, 1¾ yds of ¼"w red grosgrain ribbon, polyester fiberfill, instant coffee, 3-ply jute, thread to match fabric and jute, tracing paper, fabric marking pencil, and small crochet hook (to turn fabric).

1. Dissolve 1 tablespoon instant coffee in 1 cup hot water; allow to cool. Soak fabric in coffee several minutes. Remove from coffee and allow to dry; press.

2. Use donkey and elephant patterns and follow Transferring Patterns and Sewing Shapes, page 124, to make two donkeys and two elephants from fabric squares. Stuff shapes with fiberfill; leaving tail openings unstitched, sew final closures by hand.

3. For each tail, cut one 5" length of jute. Tie a knot 1" from each end. Insert one knotted end of jute into tail opening; whipstitch opening closed around jute.

4. Untwist end of jute in each tail; use a straight pin to separate jute.

5. Referring to photo and using thread to match jute, whipstitch donkeys and elephants together.

6. For each bow, cut one 14" length of ribbon. Referring to photo, tie ribbon in a bow around neck of donkey or elephant; trim ribbon ends.

7. For hanging loops, whipstitch one ½" long loop of ribbon to each end of string.

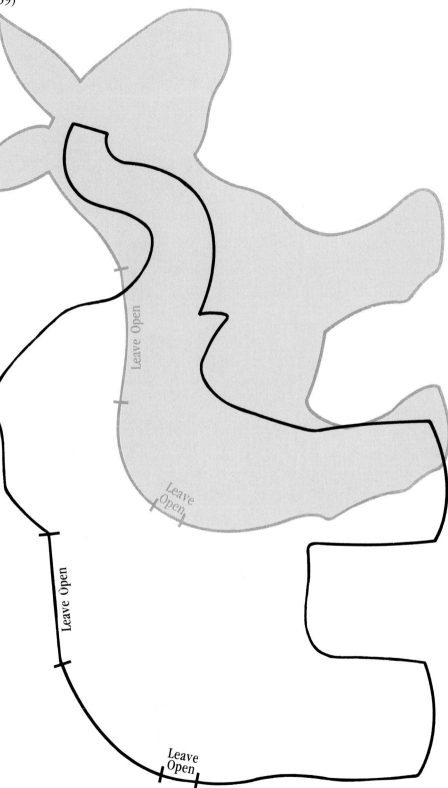

Leave Open

Leave Open

Leave Open

Leave Open

Leave Open

# HALLOWEEN

On Hallowe'en, Oh, mercy me,
The awfullest things that one can see,
Ghosts,
and goblins,
and witches too,
And other things to frighten you.

Instructions for this collection begin on page 76.

W hen witches wear smiles, Halloween takes on a gentler mood. A friendly hearth witch will still work her charm long after the goblins are gone, just like the kitchen witches that were once kept by colonial families to ensure good luck. Her brood of kitties, sewn with simple, childlike stitches, adds enchantment to the homey scene.

**F**all arrives in the midst of the earth's harvest, adding crispness to the air and setting the foliage ablaze with color. Fat pumpkins ripen just in time for Halloween carving, and we bid brave trick-or-treaters welcome with grinning jack-o'-lanterns and spooky silhouettes of witches. (When you see how easy it is to create our country pumpkin, you'll be smiling, too!)

**H**alloween is a spooky time, when bats fly at passersby and ghosts jump out with a "Boo!" Mischief plays in many ways as we decorate our homes indoors and out, preparing for treat-hungry gremlins. Our candy-stuffed pumpkin man is designed for guests to snip off a sweet for themselves.

Halloween wouldn't be complete without lots of tantalizing treats, and a paper bag full of twigs becomes a ''boo-tiful'' centerpiece when hung with spicy cookies in haunting shapes. For greeting goblins or hosting a little get-together, a charming witch and her familiar black cat (from a turn-of-the-century postcard) bring magic to a sweatshirt.

# SPOOKY COOKIE TREE  (Shown on page 74)

## TREE
*You will need* bare tree branches, black spray paint, container for tree, small pebbles or marbles to fill container, paper bag to hold container, natural-colored raffia, small amount of orange-colored raffia, Halloween Cookies (recipe follows), and needle and nylon line (for hangers).

1. Spray paint branches.
2. Fill container with pebbles. Place branches in container.
3. Place container in paper bag. Referring to photo, fold down top edge of paper bag and tie several strands of natural and orange raffia around bag. Fill top of container with natural raffia to cover pebbles.
4. For each cookie hanger, use needle to thread 8″ of nylon line through top of cookie. Knot ends of line together. Hang cookie on tree.

## HALLOWEEN COOKIES
Cookie Dough
3¼  cups all-purpose flour
  1  tablespoon baking powder
  2  teaspoons pumpkin pie spice
  ½  teaspoon ground ginger
  ½  cup butter or margarine, softened
1¼  cups granulated sugar
  1  egg
  1  teaspoon vanilla extract
  ¼  cup milk

Glaze
  2  cups confectioners sugar
  1  egg white
  2  tablespoons milk
      Paste food coloring
      Black licorice to decorate, optional

Royal Icing
  2  cups confectioners sugar
  1  egg white
      Paste food coloring

Preheat oven to 350 degrees. For cookies, combine flour, baking powder, pumpkin pie spice, and ginger in a medium mixing bowl. In a large mixing bowl, cream butter, sugar, egg, and vanilla. Add the dry ingredients alternately with the milk.

On a lightly floured surface, use a floured rolling pin to roll out dough to ⅛-inch thickness. Using Halloween cookie cutters, cut out dough. Transfer cookies to a lightly greased baking sheet. Bake 8 to 10 minutes or until very lightly browned around edges. Remove from pans and cool on wire racks.

For glaze, beat together sugar, egg white, and milk until smooth. Divide glaze and stir in food coloring to tint glaze as desired. Dip cookies in glaze.

If decorating cookies with licorice, press small pieces of licorice into wet glaze; allow to dry. If decorating cookies with royal icing, allow glaze on cookies to dry completely before decorating.

For royal icing, beat together sugar and egg white until smooth. Stir in a few drops of water if necessary to achieve a smooth consistency. Divide icing and stir in food coloring to tint icing as desired. Refer to photo and use a pastry bag fitted with a small round tip to decorate cookies as desired.
Yield: about 4 dozen 2½-inch cookies

# BAT STRING
(Shown on page 72)

*You will need* six 5″ x 9″ pieces of black fabric, rust-colored raffia, black thread, polyester fiberfill, hot glue gun, glue sticks, tracing paper, small crochet hook (to turn fabric), and fabric marking pencil.

1. Use bat pattern and follow Transferring Patterns and Sewing Shapes, page 124, to make three bats from fabric pieces. Stuff bats with fiberfill; sew final closures by hand.
2. To connect bats, cut several strands of raffia 10″ long. Keeping strands together, tie a double knot in center of strands; trim ends 2″ from knot. Referring to photo, glue ends of knotted raffia to backs of two bats. Repeat to attach remaining bat.
3. For hanging loops, glue one 2″ long loop of raffia to each end of bat string.
4. Cut several strands of raffia 18″ long and tie together in a bow. Referring to photo, glue bow to one end of bat string. Repeat for remaining end of bat string.

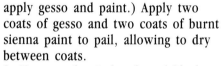

# COUNTRY PUMPKIN  (Shown on page 70)

*You will need* desired plastic jack-o'-lantern pail, medium sandpaper, gesso, burnt sienna (dk orange) and black acrylic paint, walnut water-based wood stain, matte clear acrylic spray, a soft cloth, foam brush, round paintbrush, and large stencil brush.

1. Remove handle from pail. Lightly sand outside of pail.
2. (Note: Use stencil brush and an up-and-down stamping motion to apply gesso and paint.) Apply two coats of gesso and two coats of burnt sienna paint to pail, allowing to dry between coats.
3. Use round paintbrush and black paint to paint facial features; allow to dry.
4. Working on one small area at a time, apply stain to pail and remove excess with soft cloth; allow to dry.
5. Spray pail with acrylic spray; allow to dry.

## WANDA'S CATS  (Shown on page 68)

*For each cat,* you will need two 10″ fabric squares for large cat or two ½″ squares for small cat, one 2″ fabric square for heart, two desired size buttons for eyes, colored raffia or ⅜″w satin ribbon, embroidery floss to coordinate with fabric, polyester fiberfill, and tracing paper.

1. Trace desired cat and heart patterns, on this page or page 78, onto tracing paper and cut out.
2. Place cat fabric squares wrong sides together; use cat pattern and cut two cats. Use heart pattern and cut one heart from heart fabric square.
3. For eyes, refer to photo for placement and use 3 strands of floss to sew buttons in place on one cat piece.
4. (Note: Use 3 strands of floss and Running Stitch, page 125, throughout.) Referring to grey lines on pattern, sew leg and tail lines on cat piece. Sew heart to cat piece.
5. With wrong sides facing and leaving an opening for stuffing, use a ¼″ seam allowance and sew cat pieces together. Stuff cat with fiberfill. Use Running Stitch to sew final closure.
6. Referring to photo, tie raffia or ribbon in a bow around neck.

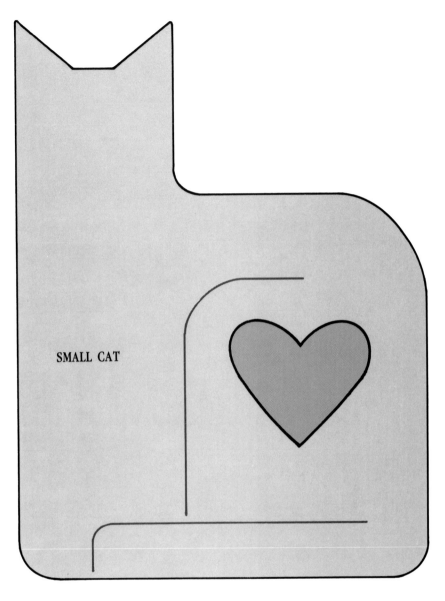

SMALL CAT

## CAT PILLOW  (Shown on page 69)

*You will need* one 10″ fabric square for cat, one 2″ fabric square for heart, two 14″ fabric squares for pillow, two desired size buttons for eyes, embroidery floss to coordinate with fabric, polyester fiberfill, and tracing paper.

1. Trace large cat and heart patterns, page 78, onto tracing paper and cut out.
2. Use patterns and cut one cat and one heart from fabric squares.
3. Follow Steps 3 and 4 of Wanda's Cats instructions on this page to finish cat.
4. Place cat on right side of one pillow piece with bottom and right edges of cat 1¾″ from edges of pillow piece. Referring to photo, use Running Stitch to sew cat in place.
5. Place pillow pieces wrong sides together. Leaving an opening for stuffing and using a 1¼″ seam allowance, use Running Stitch to sew pillow pieces together. Stuff pillow with fiberfill. Use Running Stitch to sew final closure.
6. For pillow fringe, refer to photo and clip all seam allowances at ¼″ intervals to within ¼″ of stitching line.

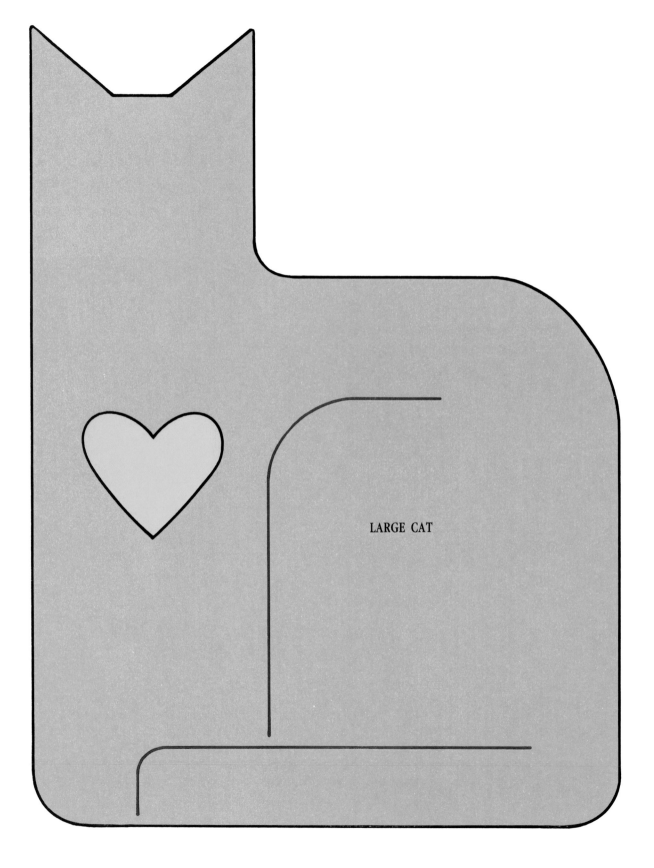

LARGE CAT

# CANDY PUMPKIN MAN (Shown on page 73)

*You will need* one 5" dia. Country pumpkin (page 76), one bundle of natural-colored raffia approx. 56" long and 6" in circumference (to measure circumference, wrap a tape measure around bundle of raffia), pair of child's scissors, 22" of orange-colored raffia or ribbon to attach scissors, candy in paper wrappers, 12" of florist wire, wire cutters, small nail, hammer, newspaper, Design Master® glossy wood tone spray (available at craft stores), hot glue gun, and glue sticks.

1. For arms, pull a 2" circumference section of raffia from bundle; cut 24" long. Tie a piece of raffia 4" from each end of section to form hands.

2. For body, pull a 4" circumference section of raffia from bundle. Fold raffia in half over center of arms; tie a piece of raffia under arms (Fig. 1).

Fig. 1

3. For waist, tie a piece of raffia 6" below arms. For legs, separate raffia into two equal parts and tie a piece of raffia around each leg 13" below waist.

4. On bottom of pumpkin, use hammer and nail to punch two holes approximately 1" apart (Fig. 2). Cut wire in half. Thread one piece of wire through holes in pumpkin. Referring to photo, wire pumpkin to body; trim ends of wire.

Fig. 2

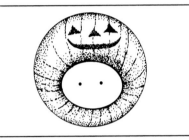

5. For hanger, insert remaining piece of wire through raffia at back of neck and twist ends together to form a loop.

6. Referring to photo, glue one end of each piece of candy to raffia.

7. Loop orange raffia or ribbon through one handle of scissors and tie to one arm (scissors will be used to snip off candy).

8. For hat, cut one 8½" x 10¾" piece from newspaper; spray both sides of newspaper with wood tone spray. Matching short edges, fold paper in half. Follow Figs. 3a and 3b to fold hat. Glue hat to head.

Fig. 3a

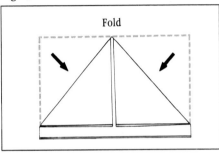

Fold

Fig. 3b

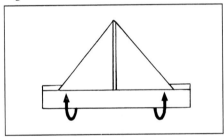

# BOO! DOORMAT (Shown on page 72)

*You will need* one approx. 14" x 24" sea grass doormat, 1⅓ yds of 44"w unbleached muslin, 1 yd of 44"w black fabric, ¼ yd of 44"w rust fabric, and #16 tapestry needle.

1. Wash and dry fabric. Cut or tear fabric from selvage to selvage into 1½" wide strips.

2. Each colored square on the chart represents one Cross Stitch. To center design, match center of mat to center of design (indicated by **C** on design). Using one fabric strip at a time, work design. Secure ends of strips on wrong

side of mat by tying ends together or by weaving under previous stitching.

3. Use one black fabric strip to Backstitch eyes.

4. To finish doormat, refer to photo and use rust fabric strips to stitch in every other hole around edge of doormat.

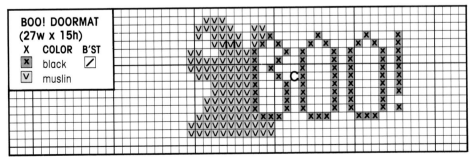

**BOO! DOORMAT (27w x 15h)**

| X | COLOR | B'ST |
|---|-------|------|
| X | black | / |
| V | muslin | |

# WANDA THE WITCH   (Shown on page 68)

*You will need* one 36"h wire tomato stand, two 9" squares and one 4½" x 8" piece of unbleached muslin, 2 yds of 44"w fabric for dress, 1 yd of 44"w fabric for pinafore, 1 yd of 44"w black fabric for hat, 1 yd of heavyweight fusible interfacing, ½ yd of paper-backed fusible web, 1⅓ yds of ¼"w grosgrain ribbon to match dress, 2⅔ yds of ¼"w grosgrain ribbon to match pinafore, natural-colored raffia approx. 60" long, thread to match fabrics and raffia, two ¾" dia. buttons to match pinafore, two ⅜" dia. black shank buttons for eyes, florist wire, black permanent marking pen with fine point, fabric marking pencil, polyester fiberfill, hot glue gun, glue sticks, tracing paper, small crochet hook (to turn fabric), thumbtack or pin, string, one 22" long stick for broom, and one small Wanda's Cat (page 77).

1. Referring to Fig. 1, bend each prong of tomato stand; wire prongs together to form a point.

Fig. 1

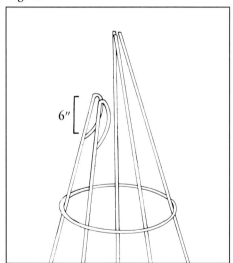

2. For head, place 9" muslin squares together and use fabric marking pencil to draw a 7" dia. circle on one square. Leaving a 2½" opening for turning (bottom of head), follow Sewing Shapes, page 124. Stuff head with fiberfill. For eyes, refer to photo and sew shank buttons to head; use marking pen to draw mouth. Insert top of stand into opening in head; glue head in place.

3. (Note: Use a ¼" seam allowance throughout unless stated otherwise.) From dress fabric, cut one 54" x 32" piece for dress and two 14" x 16" pieces for sleeves. With right sides facing and matching short edges, fold dress piece in half; sew short edges together to form a tube. Press seam open. For hem, fold one raw edge ¼" to wrong side; sew close to folded edge. For casing at neckline, fold remaining raw edge 1½" to wrong side; sew 1⅛" and ¾" from folded edge. On wrong side of fabric, make a vertical cut through one layer of casing at seamline. Turn dress right side out. Place dress on a flat surface with seam at center back.

4. With right sides facing, fold one sleeve piece in half lengthwise; sew long edges together to form a tube. Press seam open. Fold one raw edge (top) ¼" to wrong side; sew close to folded edge. For casing at wrist, fold remaining raw edge 1½" to wrong side; sew 1⅛" and ¾" from folded edge. Turn sleeve right side out. To mark center front, place sleeve on a flat surface with seam at one side; mark center front at fold. Make a vertical cut in casing through top layer of fabric at center front. Repeat for remaining sleeve piece.

5. To make top edge of one sleeve approximately 2" wide, fold top edge of sleeve into thirds; whipstitch top edge to one side of dress below casing. Repeat to attach remaining sleeve to opposite side of dress.

6. Cut one 24" length of matching ribbon for dress and two 12" lengths for sleeves. Thread each length through casing. Referring to photo, place dress over wire stand and pull ends of ribbon to gather fabric around neck; knot ribbon and trim ends. Securely tack dress to bottom of head. Lightly stuff upper part of each arm with fiberfill.

7. For hands, fold remaining muslin piece in half lengthwise; sew long edges together to form a tube. Press seam open and turn right side out. Place seam at center back of tube and press. Matching raw edges, fold tube in half and press; unfold fabric. Sew across fabric along fold line. Stuff each hand. Sew final closures by hand.

8. Referring to photo, place end of one hand 2" inside one sleeve. Pull ends of ribbon to tightly gather sleeve around hand. Tie ribbon in a bow and trim ends. Repeat for remaining sleeve.

9. From pinafore fabric, cut four 10" x 14" pieces for bodice and two 18" x 20" pieces for apron.

10. To make two bodice pieces, use bodice pattern on this page and follow Transferring Patterns and Sewing Shapes, page 124. Press bodice pieces; sew final closures by hand.

11. For apron pieces, fold short edges and one long edge of one apron piece ¼" to wrong side and press; sew close to folded edges. For gathers, baste ½" and ¼" from remaining raw edge. Repeat for remaining apron piece.

12. Pull basting threads to gather raw edge of one apron piece to fit long edge (bottom) of one bodice piece. With right sides facing, sew bodice and apron pieces together; press seam allowance toward bodice. Repeat for remaining pinafore pieces.

13. Cut eight 12" lengths of ribbon to

atch pinafore. Whipstitch lengths to
ach pinafore piece as shown in
ig. 2.

ig. 2

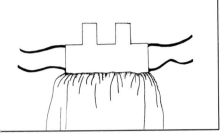

4. Overlap straps of pinafore pieces
½"; pin in place. Center one pinafore
utton on each overlapped area and
ew buttons to pinafore through all
ayers of fabric.

5. Place pinafore on witch; tie
ibbons in bows at sides and trim
nds.

6. For bangs, fold three strands of
affia in half. Use thread to tie strands
ogether approximately 6" from fold.
epeat to make six bundles. Referring
o Fig. 3, pin tied areas of bundles at
eamline of head; sew in place.

ig. 3

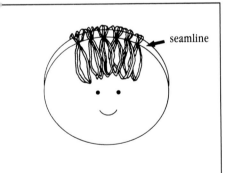
seamline

7. For hair, use thread to tie three
strands of raffia together at centers.
Repeat to make six bundles. Referring
o Fig. 4, begin at seamline of head
and pin tied areas of bundles to back
of head; sew in place.

Fig. 4

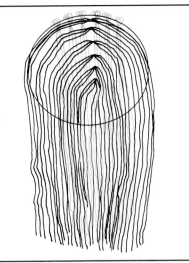

18. From hat fabric, cut one 14"
square for hat top and two 18"
squares for brim. Cut two interfacing
pieces and one fusible web piece
slightly smaller than brim pieces.

19. Follow manufacturer's instructions
to fuse interfacing to wrong sides of
brim pieces. Use fusible web and
follow manufacturer's instructions to
fuse wrong sides of brim pieces
together. Fold brim piece in half from
top to bottom and again from left to
right.

20. To mark cutting line, tie one end
of string to fabric marking pencil.
Insert thumbtack through string 7¾"
from pencil. Insert thumbtack in fabric
as shown in Fig. 5 and mark
one-fourth of a circle.

Fig. 5

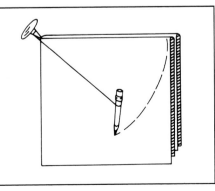

21. Following cutting line and cutting
through all thicknesses of fabric, cut
out brim. Use a medium width zigzag
stitch with a medium stitch length to
stitch over raw edges of brim.

22. For hat top pattern, cut a 14"
square of tracing paper. Insert
thumbtack through string 12¼" from
pencil. Insert thumbtack in one corner
of paper and mark one-fourth of a
circle; cut out. Use pattern and cut
one hat top from remaining black
fabric piece. With right sides facing
and matching straight edges, fold hat
top in half; sew straight edges
together. Clip corner and turn right
side out. Fold raw edge ¼" to wrong
side; press.

23. Center hat top on hat brim and
pin in place. Whipstitch edge of hat
top to brim. Securely tack hat to head.

24. (Note: Refer to photo to assemble
broom.) For broom, cut raffia 20"
long and fold in half. Insert stick into
center of raffia. Tie a piece of raffia
around broom to secure.

25. Referring to photo, place cat in
Wanda's arms; if desired, tack in
place. Place broom in one arm.

# TRICK OR TREATING BEARS   (Shown on pages 66 and 67)

Note: Use the following instructions as general guidelines for making costumes. Adjust patterns and measurements to fit your bear (we used 13″ to 20″ tall bears). Use a ¼″ seam allowance unless otherwise indicated. Refer to photo for placement of each costume on bear.

*For witch costume,* you will need orange-colored raffia, one 12″ long stick, ³⁄₁₆″w black elastic, black poster board, black fabric, purple satin fabric, 32″ of black double fold bias tape, black thread, seam ripper, stapler, hot glue gun, and glue sticks.

1. For hat brim, cut a 7″ dia. circle from poster board. Cut a 4½″ dia. circle from center of 7″ dia. circle. For hat top, cut one-half of a 10½″ dia. circle from poster board. Form into a cone shape with 4½″ dia. base; staple overlapped edges together. Insert hat top into brim and glue in place. For chin strap, place hat on bear and cut elastic to fit under bear's chin plus 1″. Glue ends of elastic to inside of hat at sides.
2. For cape, measure bear from back of neck to middle of legs and add 2″. Cut fabrics 22″ wide by determined measurement. With right sides facing and leaving an opening for turning, sew pieces together. Cut corners diagonally. Turn right side out and press; sew final closure by hand. For casing, sew 1½″ and 1″ from one long edge. Use seam ripper to open casing seams on short edges between rows of stitching. For tie, stitch long edges of bias tape together. Thread tie through casing.
3. (Note: Refer to photo to assemble broom.) For broom, cut raffia 16″ long and fold in half. Insert stick into center of raffia. Tie a piece of raffia around broom to secure.

*For vampire costume,* you will need black and orange satin fabric, 32″ of black double fold bias tape, black thread, small crochet hook (to turn fabric), tracing paper, small piece of black poster board, small gold chain, craft glue, upper section of plastic vampire teeth, elastic cord, seam ripper, and transparent tape.

1. For cape, measure bear from back of neck to middle of legs and add 4″. Cut fabrics 22″ wide by determined measurement. Sewing casing 3½″ and 3″ from one long edge, follow Step 2 of witch costume instructions to make cape.
2. Tie one end of elastic cord on each side of teeth and adjust to fit bear.
3. For eyebrows and bat for necklace, trace patterns onto tracing paper and cut out. Cut two eyebrows and one bat from poster board. Glue bat to center of chain. Tape eyebrows in place.

*For devil costume,* you will need red satin fabric, 34″ of red double fold bias tape, red thread, tracing paper, polyester fiberfill, small crochet hook (to turn fabric), and fabric marking pencil.

1. Trace horns and pitchfork patterns and black lines of tail pattern, page 83, onto tracing paper and cut out.
2. For each pattern, cut two pieces of fabric 1″ larger than pattern on all sides. Follow Sewing Shapes, page 124, to make horns, pitchfork, and tail. Stuff with fiberfill and sew final closures by hand.
3. For horns, stitch long edges of bias tape together. Center horns on tape and whipstitch in place.
4. Pin or tack tail and pitchfork to bear.

*For cat costume,* you will need black satin fabric, ³⁄₁₆″w black elastic, black thread, 1½″ dia. black pom-pom, black plastic cat whiskers, tracing paper, fabric marking pencil, small crochet hook (to turn fabric), polyester fiberfill, and craft glue.

1. For ear pattern, draw a triangle on tracing paper approximately same size as bear's ear. Add ⅜″ to all sides; cut out. Use pattern and cut four ear pieces from fabric. Fold bottom edge of each ear piece ¼″ to wrong side; press. Sew close to each folded edge. With right sides facing, sew two ear pieces together along raw edges. Turn right side out; press. Repeat for remaining pieces.
2. For nose, place pom-pom on bear's nose and cut elastic to fit around head. Tack ends of elastic to pom-pom. Cut six 3″ long whiskers. Refer to photo and glue whiskers to pom-pom.
3. For tail pattern, trace outline of grey area of tail pattern, page 83, onto tracing paper and cut out. Cut two pieces of fabric 1″ larger than pattern on all sides. Follow Sewing Shapes, page 124, to make tail. Stuff with fiberfill and sew final closure by hand. Pin or tack tail to bear.

*For mummy costume,* wrap bear in 1″ wide bandaging gauze, place a plastic spider in ear, and drape a small piece of artificial spider webbing from ear.

*For ghost costume,* drape a piece of white fabric over bear and cut holes for ears and eyes.

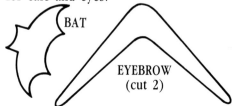

BAT

EYEBROW (cut 2)

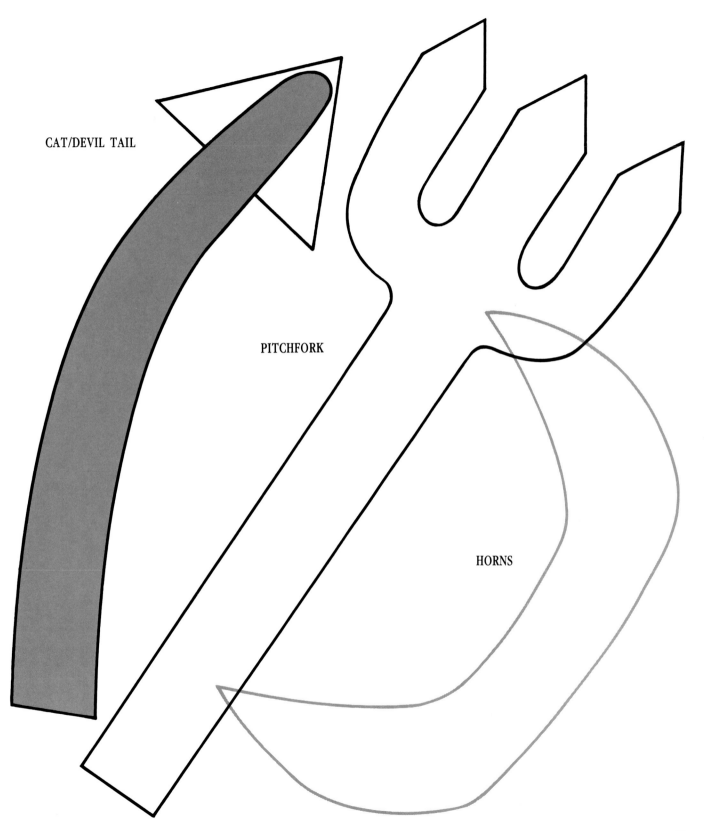

CAT/DEVIL TAIL

PITCHFORK

HORNS

# WITCH SWEATSHIRT (Shown on page 75)

*You will need* one sweatshirt, embroidery floss (see color key), #24 tapestry needle, 8″ x 9″ piece of 12 mesh waste canvas, 8″ x 9″ piece of lightweight non-fusible interfacing, masking tape, embroidery hoop (optional), tweezers, and a spray bottle filled with water.

1. Wash and dry sweatshirt. Cover edges of canvas with masking tape.
2. Refer to photo for placement of design; mark center of design on sweatshirt with a straight pin.
3. Match center of canvas to pin. Use blue threads in canvas to place canvas straight on sweatshirt; pin canvas to sweatshirt. Pin interfacing to wrong side of sweatshirt under canvas. Baste securely around edges of canvas through all three thicknesses. Then baste from corner to corner and from side to side.
4. (Note: Using a hoop is recommended when working on a sweatshirt.) Work design on canvas, stitching from large holes to large holes. Use 3 strands of floss for Cross Stitch, 1 for Backstitch, and 1 for French Knots.

5. Remove basting threads and trim canvas to within ¾″ of design. Spray canvas with water until it becomes limp. Pull out canvas threads one at a time using tweezers.
6. Trim interfacing close to design.

Design size worked over 12 mesh waste canvas — 4¾″ x 7¼″

## WITCH (57w x 87h)

| X | DMC | ¼X | B'ST | ANC. | COLOR |
|---|-----|----|----|------|-------|
| 2 | 309 | ◩ | ◩ | 042 | lt red |
| ■ | 310 | ◩ | ◩ | 0403 | black |
| ■ | 640 | | | 0393 | dk beige |
| 5 | 642 | ◩ | | 0392 | beige |
| X | 704 | | ◩ | 0256 | yellow green |
| + | 725 | | | 0306 | gold |
| ○ | 727 | | | 0295 | lt gold |
| ◇ | 754 | ◩ | | 4146 | lt peach |
| S | 758 | ◩ | | 0882 | peach |
| ▲ | 814 | | | 044 | dk red |
| ✳ | 815 | | | 043 | red |
| ☆ | 822 | | | 0390 | lt beige |
| 4 | 844 | | | 0401 | grey |
| ◐ | 918 | | | 0341 | vy dk rust |
| V | 919 | | ◩ | 0340 | dk rust |
| ▨ | 920 | | | 0339 | rust |
| △ | 921 | | | 0338 | lt rust |
| − | 962 | | | 076 | pink |
| ★ | 977 | | | 0313 | dk gold |
| ◉ | 3031 | | | 0905 | brown |
| ◑ | 3362 | | | 0263 | dk green |
| 3 | 3363 | | | 0262 | green |
| N | 3364 | | | 0261 | lt green |
| • | 310 | | | | black French Knot |

84

# FLYING WITCH WREATH (Shown on page 71)

*You will need* one 22″ dia. grapevine wreath, one 13″ square of aluminum flashing (available at hardware stores), tracing paper, utility scissors, glossy black spray paint, natural-colored raffia, dried bittersweet, purchased preserved fall leaves, grapevine twigs, florist clay, hot glue gun, and glue sticks.

1. Matching arrows to form one pattern, trace witch pattern onto tracing paper and cut out. Use pattern and utility scissors to cut witch from flashing.

2. Spray paint witch.

3. (Note: Refer to photo to assemble wreath.) Glue several twigs in wreath opening. Glue leaves and bittersweet to wreath. Tie raffia in a bow with streamers; glue to wreath.

4. Use clay to attach witch to twigs in wreath opening.

# Thanksgiving

As the sunlit days
of Indian summer slip away
and the autumn harvest is gathered in,
we give thanks for the blessings
of the year. In the midst of our
preparations, many of us
find our thoughts drawn back
to the first harvest feast
of the Pilgrim settlers.
Joined by the Indians who had
befriended them during
their first winter in the New World,
the small group had many reasons
to be thankful. Today,
we give thanks and celebrate
much as those early settlers did,
gathering family and friends
together for a special day
of fun and fellowship.

Instructions for this collection begin on page 92.

A pretty table runner brings warmth to a room. This re-creation of a traditional American handicraft is an example of the colonists' thrift and ingenuity — skillfully producing useful, attractive accessories from the tiniest fabric scraps. The pieces were often called "penny rugs" because of the round copper coins used as templates in their creation. Matching coasters (our modern adaptation) feature a maple leaf pattern. Painted with a false woodgrain and fall leaf pattern, a simple wooden box becomes a treasure chest reflecting the vibrant rusts and golden browns of autumn. Early Americans often turned to such painted finishes to dress up their plain furniture.

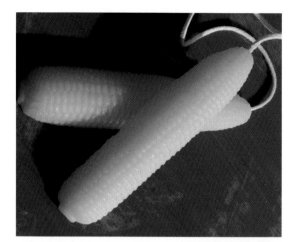

A rustic basket filled with a sampling of nature's bounty beautifully displays the muted hues of fall. A simple drying method helps the fruits retain a bit of natural color. In the spirit of our resourceful ancestors, we turned to something we had on hand — corn pone pans — to shape our beeswax candles.

A raffia-tied bundle of brilliant fall foliage greets passersby with a medley of warm ambers and rusts. Any combination of autumn materials — leaves, vines, dried fruits and vegetables, and other decorative items — can be used to reflect your personal taste.

# PENNY TABLE RUNNER (Shown on page 88)

*For an 11½" x 41" runner,* you will need ¼ yd each of the following 44"w wool fabrics: blue, beige, rust, teal, green, and maroon; ⅔ yd of 44"w black wool fabric; one 16" x 44" piece of rust wool fabric for backing; 20 skeins of dk gold embroidery floss; rust thread; fabric glue; tracing paper; and cardboard.

1. Trace each small, medium, and large circle and teardrop pattern onto tracing paper and cut out. Use patterns and cut templates from cardboard.

2. Use circle templates and cut the following number of circles from fabric:

    blue - 12 medium and 3 small
    beige - 3 medium and 12 small
    rust - 10 medium and 16 small
    teal - 16 medium and 10 small
    green - 8 medium and 10 small
    maroon - 10 medium and 8 small
    black - 59 large

3. Use teardrop templates and cut 10 large teardrops from black fabric, 10 medium teardrops from maroon fabric, and 10 small teardrops from green fabric.

4. (Note: Refer to photo for Steps 4 - 6.) To assemble "pennies," center and stack fabric circles as indicated in Diagram Key; use a dot of glue to secure each circle. To assemble a total of 10 teardrops, center and stack fabric teardrops; use a dot of glue to secure each teardrop.

5. (Note: Use 4 strands of floss and Blanket Stitch, page 125, for Steps 5 and 6.) Work Blanket Stitch around edge of each small and medium fabric circle and teardrop.

6. Refer to Diagram to arrange pennies and teardrops on backing fabric; use a dot of glue to secure each penny and teardrop. Work Blanket Stitch around edge of each large fabric circle and teardrop.

7. Cut backing fabric ¼" from outer edges of circles and teardrops. Fold fabric ¼" to wrong side and hem; press.

### DIAGRAM

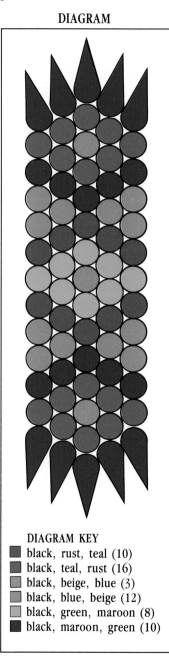

DIAGRAM KEY
- black, rust, teal (10)
- black, teal, rust (16)
- black, beige, blue (3)
- black, blue, beige (12)
- black, green, maroon (8)
- black, maroon, green (10)

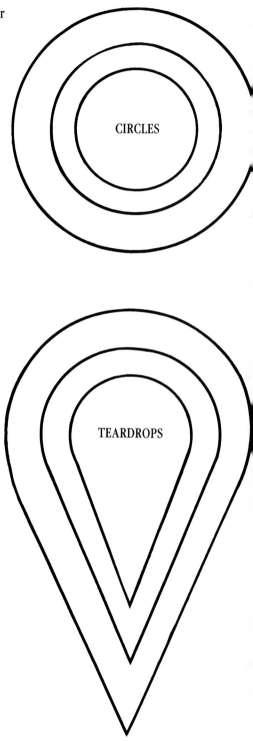

CIRCLES

TEARDROPS

# DRIED FRUIT
(Shown on page 90)

We dried fresh lemons, oranges, and pomegranates. Other fruits such as grapefruits and limes can also be dried.

It will take several weeks for the fruit to dry. It is best to begin the drying process at least six to ten weeks before the dried fruit is needed. Buy extra fruit to allow for spoilage. For best results, dry fruit when humidity is low.

To dry fruit, place on a wire rack or in a bowl in a dry place; turn fruit daily. Fruit is dried when it becomes hard and lightweight.

# PENNY COASTERS
(Shown on pages 88 and 89)

For each coaster, you will need three 5½" squares of desired colors of wool fabric, three 5" squares of medium weight fusible interfacing, tracing paper, fabric glue, and desired color of embroidery floss.

1. Follow manufacturer's instructions to fuse interfacing to wrong side of each fabric square.
2. Trace each coaster pattern onto tracing paper and cut out. Use patterns and cut one large circle, one small circle, and one leaf from fabric squares.
3. Referring to photo for placement, use a dot of glue to secure circles and leaf.
4. Use 4 strands of floss and work Blanket Stitch, page 125, around edge of each circle and leaf.

# BEESWAX CORN CANDLES  (Shown on pages 87 and 90)

Note: The small candles are for decorative use only.

For each large candle, you will need one metal corn pone pan with 5½" long sections and 6½" of candlewicking.

For each pair of small candles, you will need one metal corn pone pan with 4" long sections and 9" of candlewicking.

You will also need beeswax; double boiler or electric frying pan and a can for melting wax; newspaper; vegetable oil; and an old, small paintbrush.

Caution: Do not melt wax over an open flame or directly on burner.
1. Cover work area with newspaper.

Melt wax in double boiler over hot water or in a can placed in an electric frying pan filled with water.
2. For large candle, lightly oil two sections of pan. Pour wax into oiled sections of pan; allow wax to harden. Add more wax if needed. Remove pieces from pan and place wick along center of one piece with wick extending from top. Place flat sides of pieces together. To join, melt a small amount of wax and use paintbrush to apply wax along seam of pieces.
3. For pair of small candles, lightly oil two sections of pan. Pour wax into oiled sections of pan. Press 1" of each end of wick into top center of each piece; allow wax to harden. Add more wax if needed. Remove pieces from pan.

COASTER

## FALSE-GRAINED BOX (Shown on page 89)

*You will need* a box with molded edges (we used a 15″ x 10″ x 9″ box from Walnut Hollow Farm®); fine sandpaper; the following Folk Art® products in 2 oz. bottles: 2 bottles Harvest Gold and 1 bottle Rusty Nail acrylic paint, 1 bottle Apple Butter Brown Antiquing, 2 bottles Thickener, and 2 bottles Waterbase Varnish; fresh leaves in various sizes and shapes; 1″w foam brushes; small, round paintbrush; small dried corncob; small piece of terry cloth; pencil with eraser; tweezers; two small jars with lids; plastic wrap; and masking tape.

1. Sand box lightly. Apply one coat of varnish to box; allow to dry.
2. Apply two coats of Harvest Gold to box, allowing to dry between coats.
3. For glazes, mix ½ bottle Rusty Nail and 1 bottle Thickener in one small jar. Mix ½ bottle Apple Butter Brown Antiquing and 1 bottle Thickener in remaining jar.
4. (Note: Refer to photo for Steps 4 - 11. Practice graining techniques on scrap wood before graining box. Use tape to protect areas on box adjacent to area being grained; remove tape after grained area is dry.) For box top, work quickly and apply one coat of Rusty Nail glaze to box top so that box color barely shows through glaze. Immediately place leaves face down on box top in desired positions. Use eraser end of pencil to firmly press all areas of each leaf into glaze. After all leaves have been pressed into glaze, use tweezers to carefully lift leaves from box top; allow to dry.
5. Apply a light coat of Apple Butter Brown glaze to box top. Use a foam brush to remove excess glaze until very little remains; allow to dry.
6. For one box side, work quickly and apply one coat of Apple Butter Brown glaze to box side so that box color

barely shows through glaze.
7. For corncob pattern at bottom corners of box, place corncob at left edge of box (Fig. 1). Holding bottom of corncob in place, move top of corncob approximately ¼″ through glaze. Holding bottom of corncob in place, lift remainder of corncob out of glaze and move it forward approximately ¼″. Following arrows in Fig. 1, repeat moving and lifting motion until pattern is complete. Repeat for opposite corner on box side.

Fig. 1

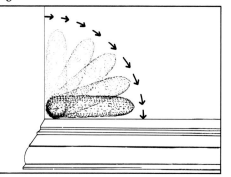

8. For mottled effect, use a crumpled piece of plastic wrap to stamp box side, stamping close to but not touching corncob patterns.
9. Using pad of index finger as a stamp, stamp fingerprints along curved edges of corncob patterns; allow to dry.
10. Repeat Steps 6 - 9 for each remaining box side.
11. For molded edges of box bottom and box top, use round paintbrush and Rusty Nail glaze to paint one groove around box bottom and two grooves around box top; allow to dry. Apply one coat of Apple Butter Brown glaze to all molded edges. Use terry cloth to stamp molded edges; allow to dry.
12. Apply two coats of varnish to box, allowing to dry between coats.

## THANKSGIVING GIFTS
(Shown on page 87)

*You will need* one 12″ x 15″ piece of Delicate Teal Jobelan (28 ct), embroidery floss (see color key, page 95), embroidery hoop (optional), and desired frame (we used a custom frame).

1. Work design over two fabric threads, using 2 strands of floss for Cross Stitch, 1 for Backstitch, and 1 for Half Cross Stitch.
2. Frame as desired.

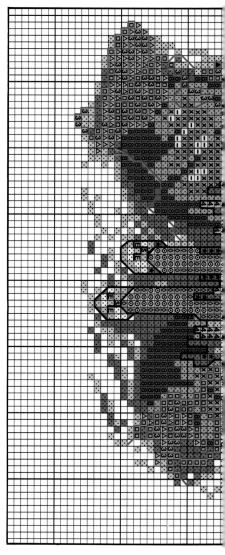

## THANKSGIVING GIFTS (77w x 119h)

| X | DMC | ¼X | ½X | B'ST | ANC. | COLOR |
|---|-----|-----|-----|------|------|-------|
| | ecru | | | | 0926 | ecru |
| | 310 | | | | 0403 | black |
| | 319 | | | | 0217 | green |
| | 347 | | | | 013 | red |
| | 367 | | | | 0216 | green |
| | 413 | | | | 0400 | blue grey |
| | 433 | | | | 0944 | lt brown |
| | 435 | | | | 0365 | dk brown |
| | 437 | | | | 0362 | tan |
| | 640 | | | | 0903 | dk tan |
| | 644 | | | | 0830 | beige |
| | 676 | | | | 0891 | lt beige |
| | 680 | | | | 0901 | yellow |
| | 739 | | | | 0366 | dk yellow |
| | 745 | | | | 0300 | lt yellow |
| | 754 | | | | 0301 | lt tan |
| | 758 | | | | 9575 | lt peach |
| | 760 | | | | 4146 | peach |
| | 761 | | | | 09 | lt pink |
| | 801 | | | | 08 | pink |
| | 807 | | | | 0359 | brown |
| | 844 | | | | 0168 | turquoise |
| | 869 | | | | 0401 | grey |
| | 890 | | | | 0906 | dk gold |
| | 921 | | | | 0218 | dk green |
| | 922 | | | | 0326 | orange |
| | 977 | | | | 0324 | lt orange |
| | 3031 | | | | 0313 | dk brown |
| | 3045 | | | | 0380 | gold |
| | 3328 | | | | 0888 | dk pink |
| | 3347 | | | | 011 | dk pink |
| | | | | | 0266 | yellow green |

Blue area indicates last row of top section of design.

## THANKSGIVING GIFTS
(77w x 119h)

| | | | |
|---|---|---|---|
| Aida 11 | 7" | x | 10⅞" |
| Aida 14 | 5½" | x | 8½" |
| Aida 18 | 4⅜" | x | 6⅝" |
| Hardanger 22 | 3½" | x | 5½" |

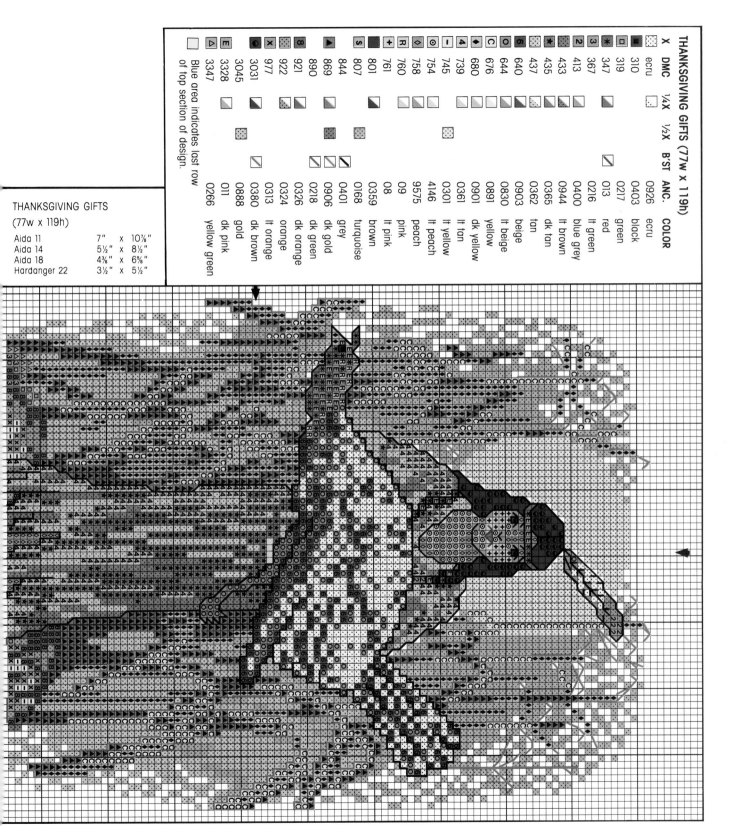

# Christmas

*Christmas in the country is a season
of simple pleasures. From
forest and fireside, tree and table —
every aroma, sight, and sound
is savored. It's a holiday
for reflecting on sacred stories,
for observing customs
begun in generations past,
and for creating new memories
to be cherished in the coming years.
But most of all, it's a wondrous
time to share with the
people you love.*

Instructions for this collection begin on page 110.

*F*or the devout Shakers, the focus of life was honest, hard work and the wise use of nature's gifts. Natural products like beeswax, garden vegetables, wild berries, and homespun fabrics sustained these people and furnished their homes. Their modest dress, simple woodworking, and heart-and-hand dedication to their way of life all gave credence to the words of the Shaker song, 'Tis the gift to be simple … 'Tis the gift to be free.

*D*uring Christmas, our thoughts turn to the Bible and its endearing characters. The familiar story of Noah herding God's creatures two-by-two into the shelter of the Ark has fascinated children throughout the ages. With charm and simplicity, a radiant sun and a sweet cookie menagerie depict the story's promising outcome.

*I*n Victorian times, luxurious fabrics and ornate trimmings gave distinctive richness to both the dress and decor of the day. This elegant style was especially evident during the holidays, when paper needlework ornaments were lavished with fancy beads, ribbon, and golden accents. Personifying the very essence of the season, the Madonna and Child were often portrayed with grandeur on Christmas cards during this era.

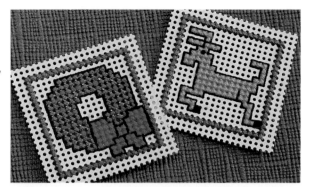

*N*o one says Noel better than Santa, especially when he's donning a sampling of merry motifs. But many of us say Merry Christmas by decorating our homes with festive table linens. Traditionally stitched all in one color in classic Nordic patterns and lovingly placed about the house, they send cheerful messages to family and friends.

*J*olly Santas dressed in richly colored robes lend an air of nostalgia to the Christmas celebration. Their chubby little figures take us back to the turn of the century when the toys that Santa Claus left often included a roly-poly or two. In those days, robes of blue or green for Santa were just as common as his familiar red suit is today.

*W*rapping paper and gift bags painted with country images evoke warm feelings of the cozy comforts of home. Even a simple, well-placed button on a gift tag brings to mind the sense of devotion found in things handmade.

*B*uilt with laughter and love, a rustic snowman radiates a childlike charm that melts our hearts. His hand-sculpted shape stirs fond memories of the frosty days of our youth when we dressed our snow creations in hand-me-down hats and scarves.

# SHAKER TREE (Shown on page 99)

## SHAKER BONNETS

*For each bonnet,* you will need one 6″ x 12″ piece of black fabric, 3″ of ¼″w black grosgrain ribbon, tracing paper, and black thread.

1. Use brim and crown patterns, page 111, and follow Transferring Patterns, page 124.
2. Use patterns and cut one brim piece and one crown piece from fabric.
3. Fold straight edge of crown piece ¼″ to wrong side and press. Baste close to folded edge. Pull basting thread to gather piece to 2″ wide; knot thread.
4. (Note: Use a ¼″ seam allowance throughout unless otherwise stated.) Baste ½″ and ¼″ from curved edge of crown piece. Pull basting threads to gather piece to fit between marks on long edge of brim piece. With right sides together, pin gathered edge of crown piece between marks on long edge of brim piece. Stitch in place.
5. Fold remaining long edge of brim piece ¼″ to wrong side; press. With right sides together, fold brim piece in half lengthwise on dotted line; stitch along each short edge. Turn brim right side out; press. Covering raw edge of crown piece with folded edge of brim, stitch through all layers close to seam.
6. For ties, fold ends of ribbon ¼″ to wrong side; press. Referring to pattern, tack ends of ribbon at **x**'s on bonnet.

## COOKIE ORNAMENTS

*You will need* Gingerbread Cookie Dough (recipe follows), paring knife, tracing paper, and needle and nylon line (for hangers).

1. Trace Shaker boy and girl patterns, page 111, onto tracing paper and cut out.
2. Place patterns on dough and use knife to cut around patterns. Bake as directed in recipe.
3. For each hanger, use needle to thread 8″ of nylon line through top of cookie. Knot ends of line together.

Gingerbread Cookie Dough

- ¼ cup butter or margarine, softened
- 3 tablespoons firmly packed brown sugar
- 2 tablespoons granulated sugar
- 3 tablespoons maple syrup
- 1½ tablespoons molasses
- 1 egg
- 2 cups all-purpose flour
- 1 teaspoon baking soda
- ¼ teaspoon salt
- ¼ teaspoon ground allspice
- ¼ teaspoon ground cinnamon
- ¼ teaspoon ground cloves
- ¼ teaspoon ground ginger

In a medium mixing bowl, cream butter and sugars. Blend in maple syrup, molasses, and egg.

In another bowl, combine flour, baking soda, salt, and spices. Stir flour mixture into creamed mixture.

Divide dough in half and wrap each half in plastic wrap. Refrigerate 2 hours.

Preheat oven to 350 degrees. On a lightly floured surface, use a floured rolling pin to roll out dough to ⅛-inch thickness. Cut out cookies as indicated in instructions. Transfer cookies to lightly greased baking sheets. Bake 8 to 10 minutes or until lightly browned. Remove cookies from pans and cool on wire racks.
Yield: about 2 dozen cookies

## HEART-IN-HAND GARLANDS

*For each garland,* you will need natural parchment paper; small, sharp scissors; craft knife; tracing paper; graphite transfer paper; removable tape; and cutting mat or thick layer of newspapers.

1. Trace heart-in-hand pattern onto tracing paper.
2. Cut one 3″ x 9″ length of parchment paper. Fold one short edge 2¼″ to one side. Using fold as a guide, fanfold remaining length of paper. Use tape to hold edges of paper together.
3. With right edge of pattern on fold, use transfer paper to transfer pattern to folded paper.
4. Place paper on mat and use craft knife to cut out small heart and areas between fingers. Cutting on solid lines only, use scissors to cut out garland.

## TREE SKIRT

*You will need* one 27″ square of unbleached muslin, black felt-tip calligraphy pen with fine point, thumbtack or pin, compass, fabric marking pencil, and string.

1. Fold fabric in half from top to bottom and again from left to right.
2. To mark outer cutting line, tie one end of string to fabric marking pencil. Insert thumbtack through string 13″ from pencil. Insert thumbtack in fabric as shown in Fig. 5, page 81, and mark one-fourth of a circle.
3. To mark inner cutting line, set compass on 1″ and place point of compass on fabric where thumbtack was inserted. Use compass to mark one-fourth of a circle.
4. Following cutting lines and cutting through all thicknesses of fabric, cut out skirt. For opening in back of skirt, cut along one fold from outer to inner edge.

5. Referring to photo and printing
1½" high letters, use pen to write
''Tis the gift to be simple...'Tis the
gift to be free...'' on skirt 1¼" from
outer edge.

**DECORATING THE TREE**
*You will also need* desired artificial
tree (we used a 4 foot tree), sets of
three mini oval Shaker boxes (the
largest box is 1½" x 2¼"),
4"h miniature ladder-back chairs,
yellow and purple dried flowers,
3½" dia. straw hats trimmed with
black ribbon, jute, 1½" x 25" piece
of burlap and florist wire for bow at
top of tree, craft glue, and nylon line
(for hangers).

Note: Refer to photo to decorate tree.

1. For each Shaker box set, stack
boxes with largest box on bottom;
glue to secure. Tie jute in a bow
around boxes.
2. For each flower cluster, tie jute in
a bow around a small cluster of the
same color of flowers.
3. For burlap bow, fringe all edges of
burlap strip ⅛". Use strip to form a
7" wide bow with 5" long streamers;
secure center of bow with piece of
jute. Wire bow to top of tree.
4. For hanger on each decoration,
thread 8" of nylon line through
decoration and knot ends of line
together.
5. Hang chairs on ends of tree
branches; hang remaining decorations
on tree. Place tree skirt around base
of tree.

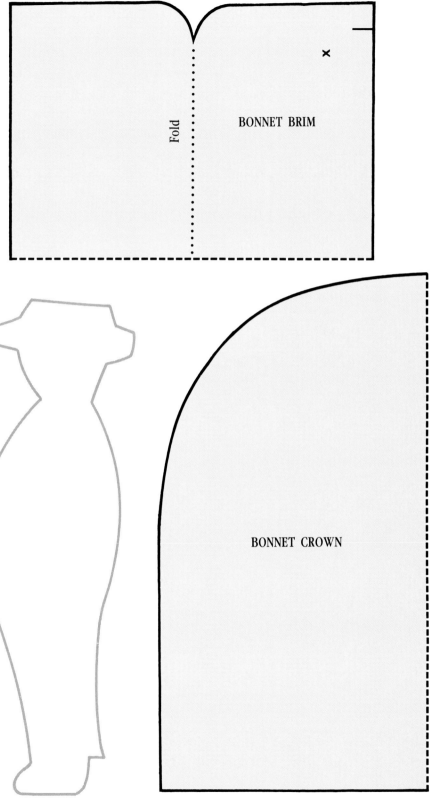

BONNET BRIM

Fold

BONNET CROWN

# VICTORIAN ORNAMENTS  (Shown on page 102)

*For each ornament,* you will need
one 6″ square of white perforated
paper (14 ct), one 5½″ square
of lightweight fusible interfacing,
embroidery floss (see color key), craft
glue, and white sewing thread.
*For ball ornament,* you will also need
8″ of ⅛″w ivory satin ribbon, 8″ of
⅛″w rose satin ribbon, 11″ of ¼″w

lace trim, and twelve 2.5 mm pearl
beads.
*For bell ornament,* you will also need
8″ of ⅛″w blue satin ribbon, one
5 mm gold bead, and eight 2.5 mm
pearl beads.
*For stocking ornament,* you will also
need 3″ of ⅛″w ivory satin ribbon
and 3″ of ⅜″w lace trim.

1. (Note: Perforated paper has a right
and wrong side. The right side is
smoother and stitching should be done
on this side.) Work design on
perforated paper, using 3 strands of
floss for Cross Stitch and 2 for
Backstitch. Refer to chart and color
key for placement of couched ribbon
or pearl beads; use white thread to

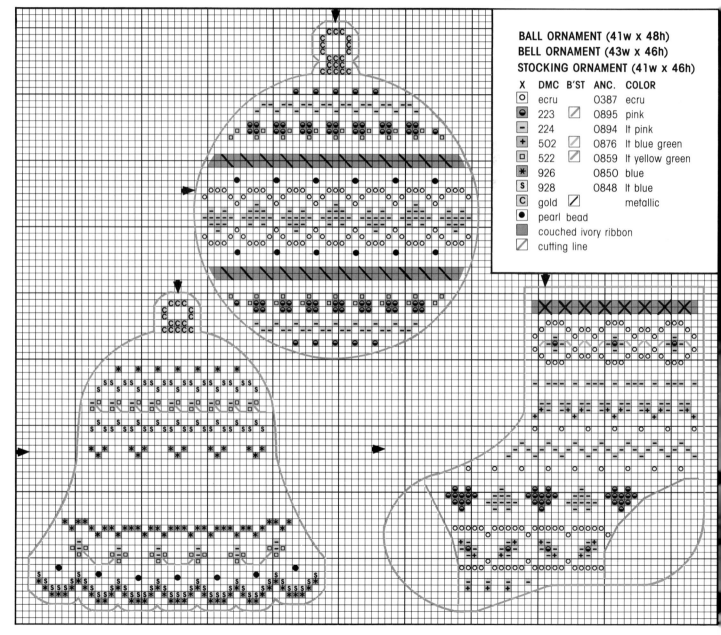

| X | DMC | B'ST | ANC. | COLOR |
|---|---|---|---|---|
| O | ecru | | 0387 | ecru |
| ◉ | 223 | ╱ | 0895 | pink |
| - | 224 | | 0894 | lt pink |
| + | 502 | ╱ | 0876 | lt blue green |
| □ | 522 | ╱ | 0859 | lt yellow green |
| * | 926 | | 0850 | blue |
| S | 928 | | 0848 | lt blue |
| C | gold | ╱ | | metallic |
| ● | pearl bead | | | |
| | couched ivory ribbon | | | |
| ╱ | cutting line | | | |

**BALL ORNAMENT (41w x 48h)**
**BELL ORNAMENT (43w x 46h)**
**STOCKING ORNAMENT (41w x 46h)**

ew pearl beads to ornament.

. Follow manufacturer's instructions o fuse interfacing to back of stitched iece. Follow grey cutting lines on hart to cut out stitched piece.

. (Note: Refer to photo for teps 3 - 6.) For ball ornament, glue ace trim on back of ball around edge. ie rose ribbon in a bow and trim nds; glue bow at top of ball.

. For bell ornament, tack gold bead nd remaining pearl bead at bottom enter of bell. Tie ribbon in a bow nd trim ends; glue bow at top of ell.

. For stocking ornament, glue lace rim on back of stocking along top dge.

. For hanger, thread 8″ of thread hrough top of ornament. Knot ends f thread together.

## COUNTRY CHRISTMAS TREE
Shown on page 97)

*You will need* branches of fresh greenery, container for branches, ebbles or marbles to fill container, lesired cookie cutters, two pieces of homespun fabric cut 1″ larger on all ides than each cookie cutter, thread to match fabric, fabric marking pencil, small crochet hook (to turn fabric), polyester fiberfill, and nylon line (for hangers).

. Fill container with pebbles. Place branches in container. Fill container with water.

. Use cookie cutters for patterns and follow Sewing Shapes, page 124, to make desired number of ornaments. Stuff with fiberfill and sew final closures by hand.

. For each hanger, thread 8″ of nylon line through top of ornament and knot ends of line together.

## NOAH'S HOMESPUN TREE  (Shown on page 100)

### TREE
*For an approx. 36″ high tree,* you will need 36″ of ½″ dia. dowel; the following lengths of ¼″ dia. dowel: 8″, 12″, 16″, and 20″; electric drill; ¼″ dia. drill bit; ¾ yd of 60″w quilted muslin; small pieces of homespun fabric; fabric glue; desired container for base; block of plastic foam to fit snugly in container; and straw.

1. For tree limbs, refer to Fig. 1 and mark placement of limbs on ½″ dia. dowel. Drill ¼″ dia. holes through ½″ dia. dowel at each mark. Insert ¼″ dia. dowels through ½″ dia. dowel (Fig. 1).

Fig. 1

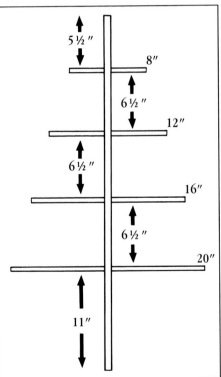

2. Cut quilted muslin into 2″ x 60″ strips. Wrap tree with approximately three layers of strips, leaving the area of tree trunk that will be inside container unwrapped. Glue ends of

strips to secure; allow to dry.

3. Tear homespun fabric into approximately 1″ x 9″ strips. Referring to photo, wrap tree with fabric strips, overlapping different colors of fabric. Glue ends of strips to secure; allow to dry.

4. Place plastic foam block in container. Insert end of tree trunk into center of foam block. Cover foam with straw.

### ANIMAL AND SUN ORNAMENTS
*You will need* Gingerbread Cookie Dough (recipe on page 110), animal cookie cutters, paring knife, six stalks of dried wheat, 3-ply jute, hot glue gun, glue sticks, and straight pins.

1. For animal ornaments, follow recipe and use cookie cutters to cut 10 pairs of animals from dough. For sun ornament, refer to photo and use knife to cut an approximately 4½″ dia. sun from dough. Bake ornaments as directed in recipe.
2. For hanger for each pair of animals, cut one approximately 15″ length of jute; tie a bow at center. Glue ends of streamers to backs of cookies.
3. For sun ornament, break stems off wheat stalks 1″ from heads. Refer to photo and glue stalks to back of sun. Cut one 10″ length of jute; glue center of jute to center back of sun.
4. Referring to photo and using straight pins, hang animal ornaments from limbs of tree. Tie sun to top of tree; trim ends of jute. Secure jute at back of tree with straight pin.

# NOAH'S ARK STOCKING AND ANIMALS (Shown on page 101)

**STOCKING**

*For stocking,* you will need two 11" x 21" pieces of fabric for stocking, one 2" x 5" piece of fabric for hanger, two 11" x 21" pieces of fabric for lining, and two 12" x 14" pieces of unbleached muslin for cuff.

*For Noah doll,* you will need two 6" x 7" pieces of unbleached muslin for doll, two 6" x 8" pieces of fabric for robe, one 2" x 10" piece of fabric for headpiece, small crochet hook (to turn fabric), polyester fiberfill, Spanish moss, and 12" of 3-ply jute.

*You will also need* thread to match fabrics, instant coffee, black permanent marking pen with fine point, tracing paper, fabric marking pencil, hot glue gun, glue sticks, and one 1¼" x 16" piece of parchment paper.

1. Dissolve 2 tablespoons instant coffee in 1 cup hot water; allow to cool. Soak 12" x 14" muslin pieces in coffee several minutes. Remove from coffee and allow to dry; press.
2. Matching arrows to form one pattern, trace stocking pattern, page 116, onto tracing paper; cut out pattern.
3. Place stocking fabric pieces right sides together. Center pattern on fabric pieces and use fabric marking pencil to draw around pattern. DO NOT CUT OUT STOCKING. Leaving top edge open, sew pieces together directly on pencil line. Leaving a ¼" seam allowance, cut out stocking. Clip curves and turn right side out.
4. For cuff, use cuff pattern, page 115, and follow Transferring Patterns, page 124. Matching long edges, fold one 12" x 14" muslin piece in half and place pattern on fold as indicated. Cut out one cuff; unfold fabric. Repeat for remaining 12" x 14" muslin piece.

5. Place cuff pieces together. Use a ¼" seam allowance and sew where indicated by dashed lines in Fig. 1a; cut notches at corners (Fig. 1a). With wrong sides together, fold cuff in half (Fig. 1b); press.

Fig. 1a

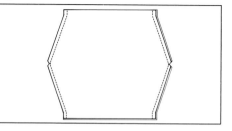

Fig. 1b

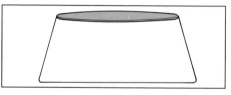

6. To attach cuff, match raw edges and place cuff inside stocking. Use a ½" seam allowance and sew raw edges together. Fold cuff to outside of stocking; press.
7. Referring to photo, use black pen to draw windows and shingles on roof.
8. For lining, use lining fabric pieces and repeat Step 3; do not turn right side out. Fold top edge of lining ½" to wrong side. With wrong sides together, insert lining into stocking; pin pieces together.
9. For hanger, fold long edges of 2" x 5" fabric piece ½" to wrong side and press. With wrong sides together, fold hanger piece in half lengthwise and press. Sew long edges together. Fold hanger in half to form a loop. Place ends of hanger between lining and stocking at right seamline with approximately 2" of hanger extending above stocking; pin in place.

10. Slipstitch lining to stocking and, at the same time, securely sew hanger in place.
11. For Noah doll, use doll pattern, page 115, and follow Transferring Patterns and Sewing Shapes, page 124. Stuff doll with fiberfill; sew final closure by hand.
12. For robe, use robe pattern, page 115, and follow Transferring Patterns, page 124. Sewing sleeve and side seams only, follow Sewing Shapes, page 124. Cut sleeves, neck, and bottom of robe on pen lines.
13. Fold bottom edge of robe ¼" to wrong side; press. Sew in place.
14. Fold sleeve and neck edges ¼" to wrong side; press. For drawstrings, use a double strand of thread and baste around sleeve and neck openings. Place robe on doll. Pull drawstrings tight around hands and neck; knot threads and trim ends.
15. For headpiece, fold headpiece fabric in half lengthwise. Referring to photo, place headpiece on head; glue to secure. Referring to photo, tie jute around robe and headpiece; trim ends.
16. For beard, refer to photo and glue a small amount of Spanish moss to face. Use black pen to draw eyes. Glue doll to stocking.
17. For list of animals, write names of animals on parchment paper. Crumple paper and then smooth flat. Referring to photo, glue list to doll and stocking.

**STUFFED ANIMALS**

*For each animal,* you will need desired cookie cutter, two pieces of fabric cut 1" larger on all sides than cookie cutter, thread to match fabric, removable fabric marking pen, and polyester fiberfill.

1. Place fabric pieces wrong sides together. Center cookie cutter on fabric pieces and use fabric marking pen to draw around cutter. DO NOT CUT OUT SHAPE. Carefully sew pieces together directly on pen line. Leaving a ⅛″ seam allowance, cut out shape. Remove marking pen lines.

2. Cut a 1½″ long slit through center back of shape; do not turn right side out. Stuff shape with fiberfill; sew final closure by hand.

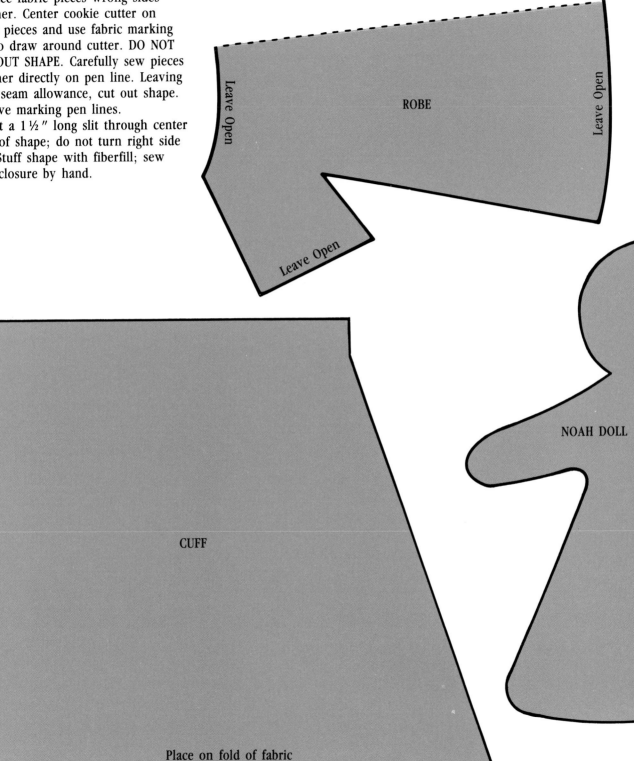

Leave Open

Leave Open

ROBE

Leave Open

NOAH DOLL

CUFF

Place on fold of fabric

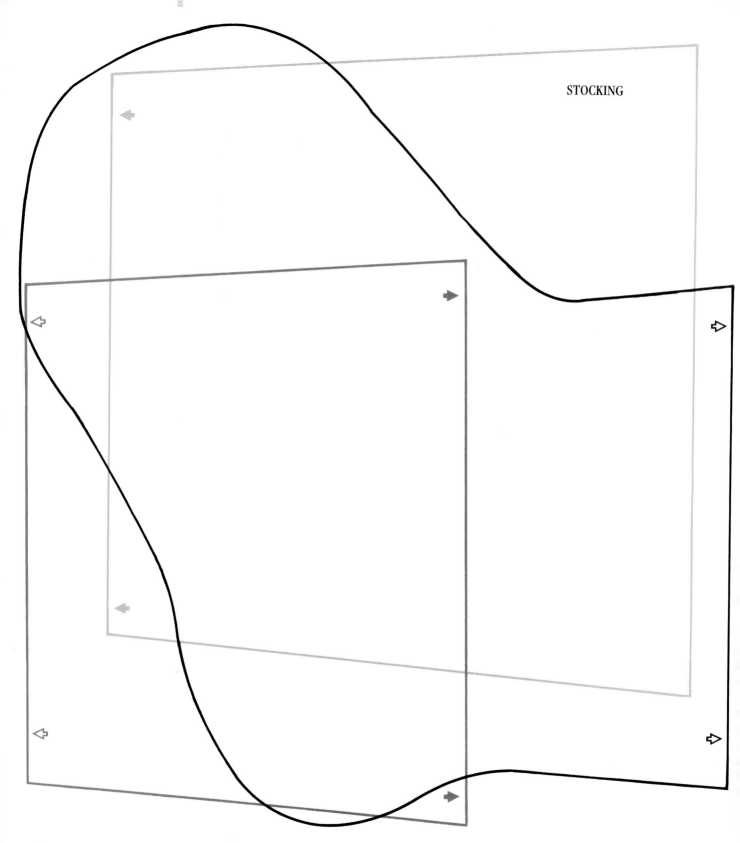

STOCKING

# OLD-FASHIONED SNOWMAN (Shown on page 109)

*You will need* 3/8 yd of 38"w unbleached muslin, one 3" x 4" piece of orange fabric, one 1" x 15" piece of fabric for scarf, thread to match fabrics, instant coffee, tracing paper, fabric marking pencil, small crochet hook (to turn fabric), polyester fiberfill, heavy thread (buttonhole twist), two 3/8"w rocks for eyes and three 1/2"w rocks for buttons, black acrylic paint, paintbrush, red embroidery floss, hot glue gun, glue sticks, transparent tape, two 5" twigs for arms, and one 1"h artificial red bird (optional).

1. Paint rocks black; allow to dry.
2. Dissolve 4 tablespoons instant coffee in 2 cups hot water; allow to cool. Soak muslin in coffee several minutes. Remove from coffee and allow to dry; press.
3. For snowman pattern, use body patterns on this page and follow Transferring Patterns, page 124. Matching arrows to form one pattern, tape patterns together.
4. Cut two 9" x 16" pieces of muslin. Use pattern and follow Sewing Shapes, page 124, to make snowman. Stuff snowman with fiberfill; sew final closure by hand.
5. To make indentations for eyes, nose, and buttons, use heavy thread to come up through snowman at one ◆; go down through snowman approximately 1/4" away. Pull thread tightly to create a dimple in snowman; knot thread and trim ends. Repeat for remaining ◆'s.
6. (Note: Use a 1/4" seam allowance throughout.) For nose, trace nose pattern onto tracing paper and cut out. Use pattern and cut one nose from orange fabric. With right sides facing and matching long edges, sew long edges of nose together. Trim seam allowance to 1/8" and turn right side out. Stuff nose with fiberfill to

within 1/2" of opening. Fold fabric over opening as shown in Fig. 1; tack folded fabric in place.

Fig. 1

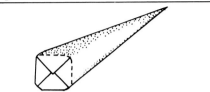

7. Referring to photo, glue rocks and nose to snowman. Use 4 strands of floss and Running Stitch, page 125, to work mouth.
8. For arms, refer to photo and cut a 1/4" long slit at each side of snowman. Apply glue to one end of each twig and insert twigs into slits.
9. For hat, cut two 3 1/2" dia. circles, two 5" dia. circles, and one 10" x 2" piece from muslin.
10. Matching right sides and short edges, sew short edges of 10" x 2" piece together to form a tube; press seam open. Fold raw edges 1/4" to wrong side; press. Turn right side out.
11. With right sides facing and leaving an opening for turning, sew 3 1/2" dia. circles together. Clip curves and turn right side out; press. Sew final closure by hand. Repeat for 5" dia. circles.
12. For crown of hat, use 2 strands of floss and large, childlike stitches to stitch one edge of tube to edge of small circle (Fig. 2). Referring to photo, center crown on remaining circle and use large, childlike stitches to stitch crown in place.

Fig. 2

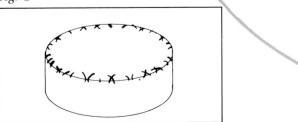

13. Referring to photo, glue hat on head; if desired, glue bird to one arm. Tie scarf fabric around neck.
14. For hanger, thread 8" of heavy thread through center back of neck and knot ends of thread together.

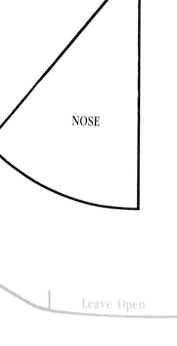

NOSE

Leave Open

# SANTA TREE (Shown on page 107)

## PAPIER MÂCHÉ SANTAS

*For each Santa,* you will need one 3" long plastic foam egg; instant papier mâché (one 1 lb. package will make approx. 12 Santas); gesso; acrylic paint (see Steps 10, 11, and 12 for colors); toothpick; a soft cloth; craft glue; foam brushes; #2, #4, and #6 flat paintbrushes; #00 liner paintbrush; 6" of 22-gauge florist wire; resealable plastic bag; and matte clear acrylic spray.

1. For hanger, bend wire in half to form a U-shape. Apply glue to ends of wire. Insert ends of wire into center of small end of egg (top), leaving 1" extended (Fig. 1); allow to dry.

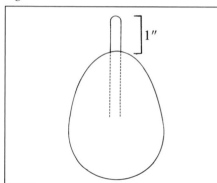

2. Following manufacturer's instructions, mix papier mâché. Store mixture in plastic bag. (Papier mâché will keep for several days in the refrigerator.)

3. Use a foam brush to apply glue to egg. Apply a smooth, ⅛" thick layer of papier mâché to egg. Leaving approximately ¼" of hanger exposed, shape additional papier mâché around hanger to form a point (Fig. 2). Allow papier mâché to dry overnight or until hard and dry.

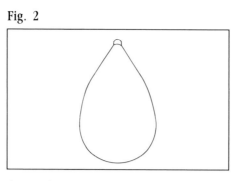

4. For face, use a pencil to draw a ⅞" x ½" oval 1" from top of Santa; for coat trim, draw a line around Santa 1½" from bottom (Fig. 3).

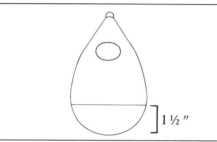

5. (Note: For Steps 5 - 8, use measurements given as general guidelines.) For beard and hair, refer to grey area in Fig. 4a and apply glue around face. Apply a ¼" thick layer of papier mâché over glued area. For mustache, refer to Fig. 4b and apply two small pieces of papier mâché at bottom of face. Use toothpick to texture beard, hair, and mustache.

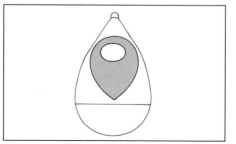

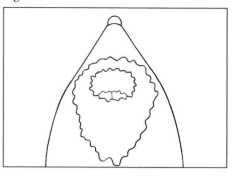

6. (Note: Refer to photo for Steps 6 - 11.) For arms, form a ⅜" thick and 1½" long roll of papier mâché. Apply a line of glue along length of roll and press glued area of roll onto body; smooth edges of roll onto body. Repeat for remaining arm.

7. For cuffs, apply a small amount of glue at end of one arm; apply a ½" wide and ⅜" thick layer of papier mâché over glued area. Repeat for remaining cuff. For coat trim, apply a line of glue along pencil line; apply a ½" wide and ⅜" thick layer of papier mâché over glued area. Use toothpick to texture cuffs and trim.

8. For hands, apply a small amount of glue below beard. Form a ⅜" dia. ball of papier mâché and press ball onto body between cuffs. Allow to dry.

9. Apply two coats of gesso to Santa, allowing to dry between coats.

10. Referring to photo, use the following colors to paint Santa:
   coat - red, blue, or green
   lower body - green, dk blue, or
      dk red
   coat trim and cuffs - light brown
   hands - black
   beard, hair, and mustache - white
   face - flesh
Allow to dry.

11. Referring to Fig. 5, use the following colors to paint face:
   cheeks - pink
   eyebrows - white
   eyes - black and blue
   eye highlights - white
Allow to dry.

Fig. 5

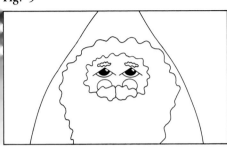

12. For stain, mix 1 part dk brown paint to 1 part water. Apply stain to Santa and remove excess with soft cloth; allow to dry.

13. Spray Santa with acrylic spray; allow to dry.

DECORATING THE TREE
*You will also need* desired artificial tree (we used a 28″ tree), basket for base of tree, desired dried materials (we used red preserved cedar, caspia, red and green eucalyptus, and red canella berries), approx. 12″ long twigs cut from a grapevine wreath, red Paper Capers™ twisted paper, florist wire, wire cutters, hot glue gun, and glue sticks.

Note: Refer to photo to decorate tree.

1. Place tree in basket.

2. Use a short piece of wire to attach each Santa to tree.

3. Arrange dried materials in tree; glue to secure.

4. Place twigs among branches.

5. For garland, cut 1½″ wide lengths of untwisted paper. Drape garland around tree.

# MADONNA AND CHILD  (Shown on page 103)

*You will need* one 9″ x 11″ piece of Tea Dyed Irish Linen (28 ct), embroidery floss (see color key), embroidery hoop (optional), and desired frame (we used an antique frame with a 3⅝″ x 4⅞″ opening).

1. Follow Working On Linen, page 125, to work design over two fabric threads. Use 2 strands of floss for Cross Stitch and 1 for Backstitch.

2. Frame as desired.

| MADONNA AND CHILD (44w x 64h) | | |
|---|---|---|
| Aida 11 | 4″ | x 5⅞″ |
| Aida 14 | 3¼″ | x 4⅝″ |
| Aida 18 | 2½″ | x 3⅝″ |
| Hardanger 22 | 2″ | x 3″ |

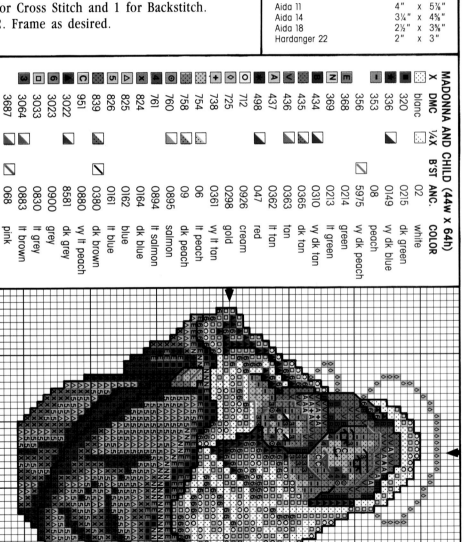

| X | ¼X | B'ST | DMC | ANC. | COLOR |
|---|---|---|---|---|---|
|  |  |  | blanc | 02 | white |
|  |  |  | 320 | 0215 | dk green |
|  |  |  | 336 | 0149 | vy dk blue |
|  |  |  | 353 | 08 | peach |
|  |  |  | 356 | 5975 | vy dk peach |
|  |  |  | 368 | 0214 | green |
|  |  |  | 369 | 0213 | lt green |
|  |  |  | 434 | 0310 | vy dk tan |
|  |  |  | 435 | 0365 | dk tan |
|  |  |  | 436 | 0363 | tan |
|  |  |  | 437 | 0362 | lt tan |
|  |  |  | 498 | 047 | red |
|  |  |  | 712 | 0926 | cream |
|  |  |  | 725 | 0298 | gold |
|  |  |  | 738 | 0361 | vy lt tan |
|  |  |  | 754 | 06 | lt peach |
|  |  |  | 758 | 09 | dk peach |
|  |  |  | 760 | 0895 | salmon |
|  |  |  | 761 | 0894 | lt salmon |
|  |  |  | 824 | 0164 | dk blue |
|  |  |  | 825 | 0162 | blue |
|  |  |  | 826 | 0161 | lt blue |
|  |  |  | 839 | 0380 | dk brown |
|  |  |  | 951 | 0880 | vy lt peach |
|  |  |  | 3022 | 8581 | dk grey |
|  |  |  | 3023 | 0900 | grey |
|  |  |  | 3033 | 0830 | lt grey |
|  |  |  | 3064 | 0883 | lt brown |
|  |  |  | 3687 | 068 | pink |

# TABLE LINENS (Shown on page 105)

Note: Table linens were stitched on Cracked Wheat Ragusa (14 ct) over 2 fabric threads, using 6 strands of floss for Cross Stitch.

*For a 13¾" x 36" table runner,* you will need one 15¾" x 36" piece of Cracked Wheat Ragusa (14 ct), embroidery floss (DMC 304 or Anc. 047), embroidery hoop (optional), and thread to match fabric.

1. With design centered and bottom of design 3" from one short edge of fabric, work design; repeat as necessary to within 1½" of each long edge. Repeat for remaining short edge.
2. Fold long edges of fabric ½" to wrong side; press. Fold ½" to wrong side again and hem. For fringe, machine stitch 2¼" from each short edge and pull out threads up to machine-stitched lines.

*For a 10" x 18¾" bread cloth,* you will need one 12" x 18¾" piece of Cracked Wheat Ragusa (14 ct), embroidery floss (DMC 304 or Anc. 047), embroidery hoop (optional), and thread to match fabric.

1. Bread cloth design is between grey lines on chart. With design centered and bottom of design 1½" from one short edge of fabric, work design; repeat as necessary to within 1½" of each long edge.
2. To finish edges, follow Step 2 of Table Runner instructions, machine stitching 1" from each short edge.

*For each 1¼" dia. napkin ring,* you will need one 4¾" x 7" piece of Cracked Wheat Ragusa (14 ct), embroidery floss (DMC 304 or Anc.047), one 2" x 6" piece of buckram or lightweight cardboard, and thread to match fabric.

1. With napkin ring design centered between long edges of fabric and beginning ½" from left short edge, work design; repeat as necessary to within ½" of right short edge.
2. Center buckram on wrong side of stitched piece. Fold short edges of fabric over buckram; pin in place. Fold one long edge of fabric over buckram; pin in place. Fold remaining edge of fabric ¼" to wrong side; fold over buckram and pin in place. Whipstitch fabric in place; remove pins.
3. Whipstitch short edges together to form a ring.

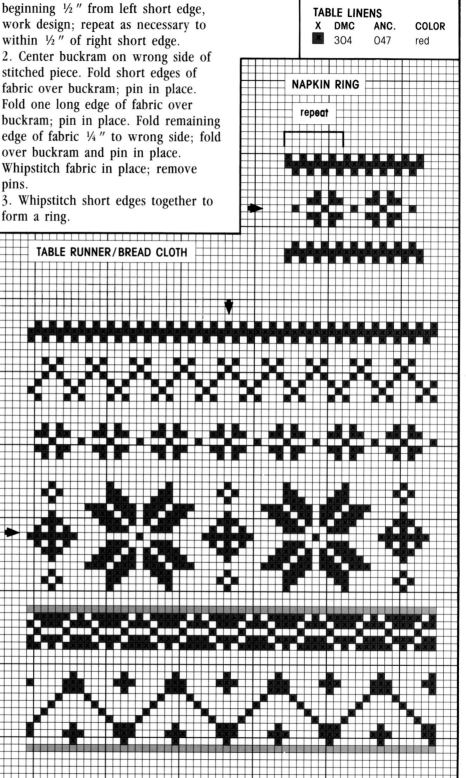

| TABLE LINENS | | | |
|---|---|---|---|
| X | DMC | ANC. | COLOR |
| ■ | 304 | 047 | red |

NAPKIN RING

repeat

TABLE RUNNER/BREAD CLOTH

# GIFT WRAPS (Shown on page 108)

*For House Gift Bag,* you will need one 6" x 11" paper lunch bag, black construction paper, tagboard (manila folder), craft knife, tracing paper, craft glue, graphite transfer paper, small stencil brush, blue acrylic paint, paper towels, two mini spring-type clothespins, and removable tape (optional).

1. Referring to photo, use house gift bag pattern and follow Stenciling, page 124, to stencil bag.
2. Cut 1¼" from top of bag. Fold top of bag 3" to front. Cut one 3¼" x 6¼" piece of construction paper; glue to folded area of bag.
3. Cut two 1" x 1⅞" pieces of construction paper; glue to clothespins. Referring to photo, pin clothespins to bag.

*For Roller Gift Wrap,* you will need one pair of shoe insoles with rubber backing, 3"w trim paint roller with 1" dia. low-nap roller cover, tracing paper, permanent felt-tip pen with fine point, wooden spool or small scrap of wood, rubber cement, foam brushes, desired colors of acrylic paint, and wrapping paper.

1. Trace roller gift wrap patterns onto tracing paper and cut out. On cloth side of one insole, use pen to draw around two houses and one heart; cut out.
2. (Note: Refer to photo for Steps 2 - 4.) With bottom of house ¾" from one side of roller, use rubber cement to glue cloth side of one house to roller. Leaving approximately ⅝" between houses, repeat for remaining house. For heart stamp, glue cloth side of heart to one end of spool.
3. For one row of houses, apply a thin coat of paint to houses and roll roller slowly across paper. Leaving approximately 2" between each row,

repeat for desired number of rows. Allow to dry.
4. Apply a thin coat of paint to heart; stamp hearts as desired.

*For Spatter Gift Wrap,* you will need wrapping paper, desired color acrylic paint, toothbrush, a small piece of screen wire, and newspaper.

1. (Note: Cover work area with newspaper and protect clothing from paint.) Place wrapping paper on newspaper.
2. To spatter paint, dip toothbrush in paint and pull bristles across edge of screen wire. Repeat to spatter desired amount of paint on paper. Allow to dry.

*For Spatter Gift Card,* you will need two sheets of white stationery, one 2¾" x 3¼" piece of Spatter Gift Wrap with pinked edges, tracing paper, thread, desired button, and craft glue.

1. For card, cut one 6½" x 7" piece of stationery. Matching short edges, fold in half; matching short edges, fold in half again.
2. Center and glue gift wrap to front of card.
3. Trace heart pattern onto tracing paper and cut out. Use pattern and cut one heart from remaining piece of stationery.
4. Referring to photo, glue heart to front of card; sew button on card.

HOUSE GIFT BAG

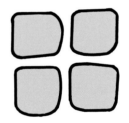

ROLLER GIFT WRAP

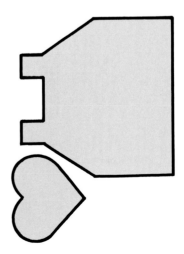

# NOEL SANTA

(Shown on pages 104 and 105)

## WALL HANGING

*For a 16" x 26" wall hanging,* you will need one 18" x 27¾" piece of Floba (18 ct), embroidery floss (see color key), embroidery hoop (optional), sewing thread to match fabric, and one 17" length of ½" dia. dowel and two end caps stained or painted desired color.

1. Work design over two fabric threads using 6 strands of floss for Cross Stitch, 2 for Backstitch, and 2 for French Knot.
2. For wall hanging, fold side edges of fabric ½" to wrong side and press; fold ½" to wrong side again and hem. For casing, fold top edge ¼" to wrong side and press; fold 1½" to wrong side and hem. For fringe, machine stitch 3½" from bottom edge and pull out threads up to machine-stitched line.
3. Insert dowel through casing and attach end caps.

## PAPER DECORATIONS

Note: Paper decorations may be used as gift tags or tree ornaments by gluing ribbons or strings for hangers on backs of decorations.

*For each paper decoration,* you will need one 3" square of cream perforated paper (14 ct) and embroidery floss (see color key).

1. (Note: Perforated paper has a right and wrong side. The right side is smoother and stitching should be done on this side.) Work desired motif including border on perforated paper; use 3 strands of floss for Cross Stitch, 2 for Backstitch, and 2 for French Knot.
2. Trim paper ⅛" (two holes) from edge of design on all sides.

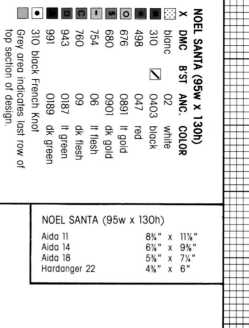

| X | DMC | B'ST | ANC. | COLOR |
|---|---|---|---|---|
| | blanc | | 02 | white |
| | 310 | ◢ | 0403 | black |
| | 498 | | 047 | red |
| | 676 | | 0891 | lt gold |
| | 680 | | 0901 | dk gold |
| | 754 | | 06 | lt flesh |
| | 760 | | 09 | dk flesh |
| | 943 | | 0187 | lt green |
| | 991 | | 0189 | dk green |

310 black French Knot

Grey area indicates last row of top section of design.

**NOEL SANTA (95w x 130h)**

| | | |
|---|---|---|
| Aida 11 | 8¾" | x 11⅞" |
| Aida 14 | 6⅞" | x 9⅜" |
| Aida 18 | 5⅜" | x 7¼" |
| Hardanger 22 | 4⅜" | x 6" |

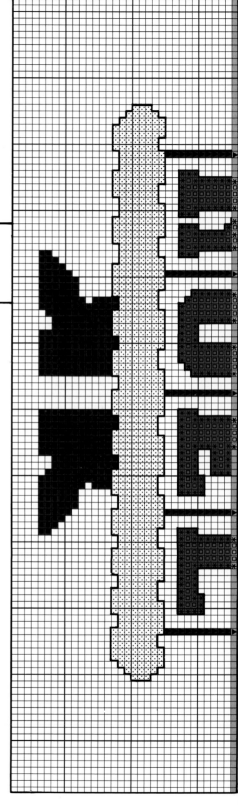

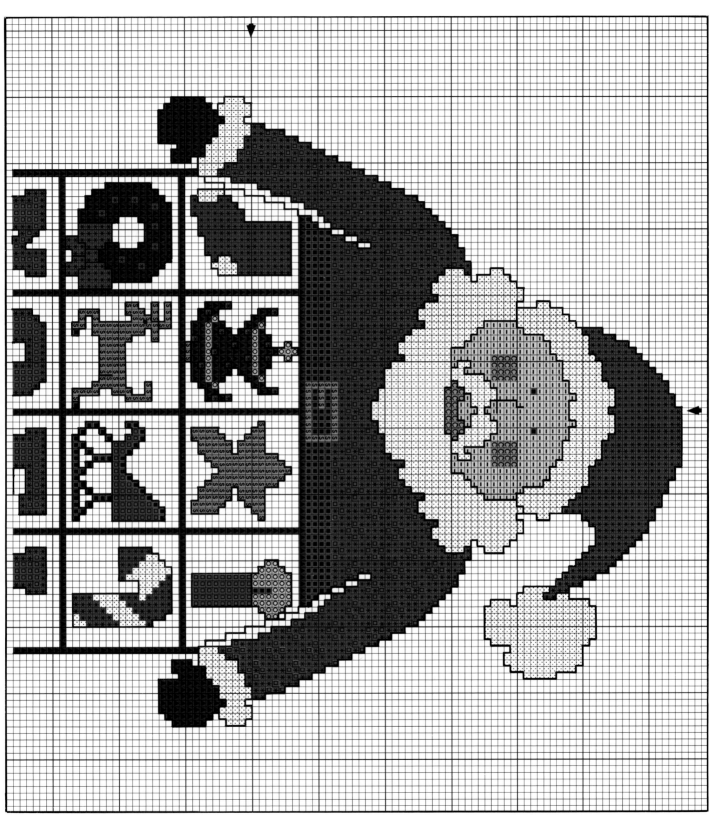

123

# GENERAL INSTRUCTIONS

## TRANSFERRING PATTERNS

*When entire pattern is shown,* place a piece of tracing paper over pattern and trace pattern, marking all placement symbols and openings. Cut out traced pattern.

*When one-half of pattern is shown,* fold tracing paper in half and place folded edge along dashed line of pattern. Trace pattern, marking all placement symbols and openings. Cut out traced pattern; open pattern and lay it flat.

## SEWING SHAPES

1. Center pattern on wrong side of one piece of fabric and use a fabric marking pencil to draw around pattern. If indicated on pattern, mark opening for turning. DO NOT CUT OUT SHAPE.
2. With right sides facing and leaving an opening for turning, carefully sew fabric pieces together *directly on pencil line.*
3. Leaving a ¼ ″ seam allowance, cut out shape. Clip seam allowance at curves and corners. Turn shape right side out. Use the rounded end of a small crochet hook to completely turn small areas.
4. If pattern has facial features or detail lines, use fabric marking pencil to lightly mark placement of features or lines.

## STENCILING

1. Trace pattern onto tracing paper. Using transfer paper, center and transfer design to tagboard. Use craft knife to cut out stencil.
2. (Note: Use removable tape to mask all areas on stencil next to area to be painted.) Hold or tape stencil in place while stenciling. Use a clean, dry stencil brush for each color of paint. Dip brush in paint and remove excess paint on a paper towel. Brush should be almost dry to produce a good design.
3. Beginning at edge of cut out area, apply paint in a stamping motion. Shade design by applying more paint around edge than in center. Allow paint to dry slightly and remove stencil.

## CROSS STITCH

### COUNTED CROSS STITCH

Work one Cross Stitch to correspond to each colored square on the chart. For horizontal rows, work stitches in two journeys (Fig. 1). For vertical rows, complete each stitch as shown in Fig. 2. When working over two fabric threads, work Cross Stitch as shown in Fig. 3. When the chart shows a Backstitch crossing a colored square (Fig. 4), a Cross Stitch (Fig. 1, 2, or 3) should be worked first; then the Backstitch (Fig. 8, page 125) should be worked on top of the Cross Stitch.

Fig. 1

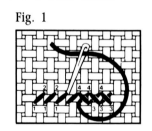

Fig. 2

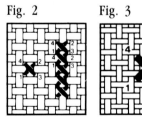

Fig. 3

Fig. 4

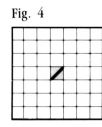

QUARTER STITCH (¼ X)
Quarter Stitches are denoted by triangular shapes of color on the chart and on the color key. Come up at 1 (Fig. 5); then split fabric thread to go down at 2. Fig. 6 shows this technique when working over two fabric threads.

Fig. 5

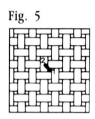

Fig. 6

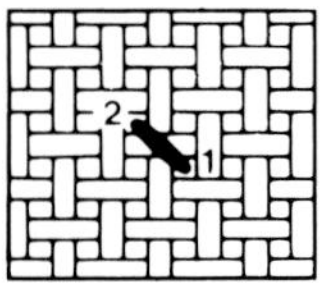

HALF CROSS STITCH (½ X)
This stitch is one journey of the Cross Stitch and is worked from lower left to upper right. Fig. 7 shows the Half Cross Stitch worked over two fabric threads.

Fig. 7

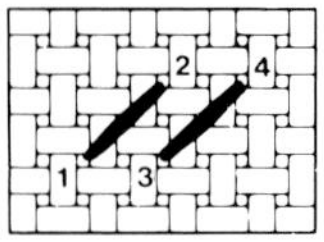

# ACKSTITCH

or outline detail, Backstitch (shown
n chart and on color key by black or
olored straight lines) should be
worked after the design has been
ompleted (Fig. 8).

Fig. 8

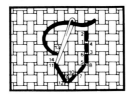

# RENCH KNOT

Bring needle up at 1. Wrap thread
once around needle and insert needle
t 2, holding end of thread with
on-stitching fingers (Fig. 9). Tighten
knot; then pull needle through fabric,
holding thread until it must be
eleased. For a larger knot, use more
trands; wrap only once.

Fig. 9

# WORKING ON LINEN

Using a hoop is optional when
working on linen. Roll excess fabric
rom left to right until stitching area is
n the proper position. Use the sewing
method instead of the stab method
when working over two fabric
threads. To use the sewing method,
keep your stitching hand on the right
ide of the fabric; take the needle
down and up with one stroke (the
tab method uses two strokes). To add
upport to stitches, place the first
Cross Stitch on the fabric with
titch 1-2 beginning and ending where
a vertical fabric thread crosses over a

horizontal fabric thread (Fig. 10).

Fig. 10

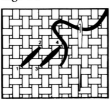

# EMBROIDERY

## BLANKET STITCH

Referring to Fig. 1a, come up at 1. Go
down at 2 and come up at 3, keeping
the thread below the point of the
needle. Continue working in this
manner, going down at even numbers
and coming up at odd numbers
(Fig. 1b).

Fig. 1a

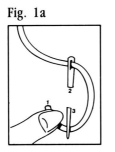

Fig. 1b

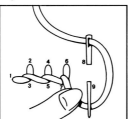

# RUNNING STITCH

Referring to Fig. 2, make a series of
straight stitches with stitch length
equal to the space between stitches.

Fig. 2

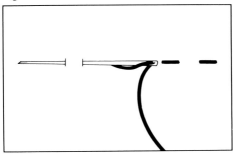

# CROCHET

## WORKING INTO THE CHAIN

When working into the beginning
chain of a crochet project, insert hook
*into the ridge* at back of each chain
(Fig. 1).

Fig. 1

## WORKING INTO ROWS

When working into rows of a crochet
project, insert hook *under* the V of
each stitch (Fig. 2). Be sure to pick up
both loops.

Fig. 2

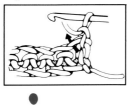

Continued on page 126

# GENERAL INSTRUCTIONS (continued)

## DOUBLE CROCHET

To begin a double crochet, hook yarn once over hook, bringing yarn from back over top of hook. Insert hook into ridge of chain or under V of stitch. Hook yarn and draw through. There should now be three loops on hook (Fig. 3). Hook yarn again and draw through the first two loops on hook (Fig. 4). Two loops should remain on hook. Hook yarn again and draw through remaining two loops (Fig. 5). One double crochet is now complete.

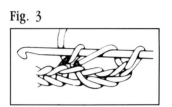

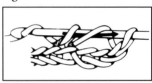

## QUILTING

### QUILTING STITCH

1. Thread quilting needle with an 18" length of quilting thread; knot one end of thread.

2. Bring needle up through all layers of fabric and batting; when knot catches on back of quilt, give thread a quick, short pull to pop knot through fabric into batting (Fig. 1).

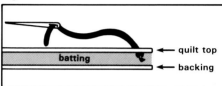

3. To quilt, use small running stitches that are equal in length (Fig. 2).

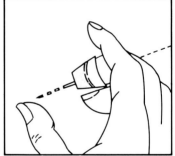

4. At the end of a length of thread, knot thread and take needle down through layered fabric and batting; when knot catches on top of quilt, pop knot through fabric into batting. Clip thread close to fabric.

### APPLYING BINDING

1. For binding, match wrong sides and raw edges and fold bias strip in half lengthwise; press. Fold long raw edges to center; press.

2. Open one end of binding; press end ¼" to wrong side. Unfold one long edge of binding. Beginning with pressed end and matching right sides and raw edges, pin binding to edges of quilt top. Continue around quilt top until ends of binding overlap.

3. Using pressed line as a guide, sew binding to quilt (Fig. 3).

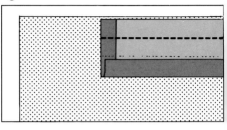

4. Fold binding over raw edges to back of quilt; whipstitch in place.

# CREDITS

We want to extend a warm thank you to the generous people who allowed us to photograph our projects in their homes.

**Valentine's Day:** John and Connie Bush
**Easter:** Joan Gould
**Mother's Day/Father's Day:** Gordon and Kelly Holt
**Patriotic Days:** Carl and Monte Brunck
**Thanksgiving:** Richard and Joan Rechtin
**Christmas:** Carl and Monte Brunck; Joan Gould

We especially thank the Department of Arkansas Heritage for allowing us to photograph portions of our **Halloween** and **Thanksgiving** collections in the Arkansas Territorial Restoration.

To Magna IV Engravers of Little Rock, Arkansas, we say thank you for the superb color reproduction and excellent pre-press preparation.

We want to especially thank photographers Ken West and Larry Pennington of Peerless Photography, Little Rock, Arkansas, for their time, patience, and excellent work.

To the talented designers who helped in the creation of many projects in this book, we extend a special word of thanks.

*An Irish Blessing*, page 27: Terrie Lee Steinmeyer
*Easter Lambs*, page 44, and *Papier Mâché Santas*, page 118:
    Linda Lindquist Baldwin
*Sweethearts*, page 45; *Witch Sweatshirt*, page 84; and *Thanksgiving Gifts*,
    page 94: Needlework adaptations by Kathy Rose Bradley
*Noel Santa*, page 122: Polly Carbonari
*Madonna and Child*, page 119: Needlework adaptation by Carol Emmer
*Victorian Ornaments*, page 112: Patricia Nasers

We extend a sincere thank you to all the people who assisted in making and testing the projects in this book: Andrea Ahlen, Trisa Bakalekos, Caren Beard, Jean Black, Jennie Black, Margaret Bredlow, Kim Camp, Trisha Duncan, Miriam Durrett, Kathy Elrod, Judy Hicks, Karen Jackson, Ginny Kopper, Melanie Long, Martha Nolan, Ray Ellen Odle, Dave Ann Pennington, Frances Reichert, Catherine Spann, Karen Tyler, and Janet Yearby.